Gay Su Pinnell
Irene C. Fountas

The **Continuum** of
Literacy Learning
Teaching Library

User Guide

GRADES
PreK–2

Heinemann
Portsmouth, NH

Heinemann
361 Hanover St.
Portsmouth, NH 03801-3912
www.heinemann.com

Offices and agents throughout the world.

"Dedicated to Teachers" is a trademark of Greenwood Publishing Group, Inc.

The author and publisher would like to thank those who have generously given permission to reprint borrowed material:

The Continuum of Literacy Learning Teaching Library User Guide, Grades PreK-2

ISBN 10: 0-325-04229-2
ISBN 13: 978-0-325-04229-9

5 4 3 2 1 SR 11 12 13 14 15

6/8/12

Introduction

The Continuum of Literacy Learning Teaching Library: Professional Development Teaching Collection, Grades PreK–2 and *The Continuum of Literacy Learning Teaching Library User Guide* are designed to help you begin thinking and talking about the enormous amount of literacy and language learning that children accomplish between the time they enter prekindergarten, to the end of second grade. One of the goals of the Continuum is to provide teachers, administrators, literacy coaches, and staff developers with a common vision for literacy learning across the grades. By providing a specific body of understandings that students in prekindergarten through grade 2 should acquire to become increasingly efficient users of oral and written language, the Continuum is a tool for both planning and assessment. With this set of eight DVDs, you will join us as we visit classrooms where teachers have designed instruction based on this comprehensive view of literacy education. Whether you are using this tool as an individual, in a small study group, or as a staff developer, you will have the opportunity to look closely at student behaviors and the teaching moves that support students in increasing their ability to talk, read, and write in several different instructional contexts.

—Irene Fountas and Gay Su Pinnell

Content and Organization of the Teaching Library

There are currently three different volumes of the Continuum: *The Continuum of Literacy Learning, Grades PreK–2; The Continuum of Literacy Learning, Grades PreK–8;* and *The Continuum of Literacy Learning, Grades 3–8*. While each volume contains much of the same material, the organization is slightly different in each to accommodate the user. To use this DVD set, you will want to have on hand either *The Continuum of Literacy Learning, Grades PreK–8* or *The Continuum of Literacy Learning, Grades PreK–2*.

The sequence of this Teaching Library and the User Guide is organized according to *The Continuum of Literacy Learning, Grades PreK–8*, with the exception of a special section on assessment on DVD 1. Assessment is the first topic in the Teaching Library because assessment is the most powerful tool in designing effective instruction, and because it provides a foundation for the close observation of the behaviors of students, which will impact the way each teaching segment in the Teaching Library is viewed. As you watch the segments and follow the sequence of learning offered in the User Guide, you will see how each continuum can be used as a tool for authentic assessment as students engage in the kinds of reading, writing, and talking they will be expected to do in the real world.

In *The Continuum of Literacy Learning, Grades PreK–8*, each instructional context is presented separately in a sequence. The tabs allow you to easily locate the context in which you are interested. Within a section, continua for grade levels are presented in order, from prekindergarten to grade 8. The last section presents the Guided Reading continuum, organized by text levels A to Z. See the inside front cover and the introductory materials in *The Continuum of Literacy Learning, Grades PreK–8*, for a more detailed description of the content and organization of each section.

In keeping with this sequence, the Teaching Library includes the following topics on each DVD:

DVD 1: Introduction and Assessment

DVD 2: Interactive Read-Aloud and Literature Discussion

DVD 3: Shared and Performance Reading

DVD 4: Writing About Reading

DVD 5: Writing: Focus on Interactive Writing

DVD 6: Writing: Focus on Writing Workshop

DVD 7: Phonics, Spelling, and Word Study

DVD 8: Guided Reading

The Continuum of Literacy Learning, Grades PreK–2 contains the same content in each section but is organized by grade level. The tabs let you turn to the grade level in which you are interested. In each grade level section, you will find all of the instructional contexts for the grade level. This continuum is designed to be most helpful as a tool for classroom teachers, prek–2, while *The Continuum of Literacy Learning, Grades PreK–8* is designed for educators working with a wider range of grade levels. The different volumes, however, can be used interchangeably as they contain the same information. You may notice that the Oral, Visual, and Technological Communication continuum is not included here. You will find that the competencies students need to develop are integrated in the reading and writing sections. You might want to take a good look at the critical areas addressed in this section and notice the opportunities in reading and writing clips.

Each individual DVD includes an introduction to the highlighted instructional context, teaching segments for the range of grade levels, and a section for PDF Resources when available. The video segments are offered with and without commentary, giving you the opportunity to first think on your own and/or with your colleagues about the reading and writing behaviors of the students and instructional moves of the teacher before listening to the comments of the authors. In

The Continuum of Literacy Learning Teaching Library, PreK–2: User Guide

addition to the commentary offered by the authors, you will notice that each clip with commentary also displays selected bulleted behaviors from *The Continuum of Literacy Learning* as they are demonstrated by students or supported by the teacher in each segment. The PDF Resources section provides materials to support your viewing as well as extend your thinking through activities suggested in the Extend sections of the User Guide. See the document *DVD at a Glance* in the appendix of this guide for a more detailed description of the contents of each DVD.

For more information about the organization of the Continuum and the DVD Collection, you will want to read the introductory materials in your version of *The Continuum of Literacy Learning, Grades PreK–8* or *The Continuum of Literacy Learning, Grades PreK–2* and view the introduction on DVD 1.

How to Use the Teaching Library and User Guide

The Continuum of Literacy Learning Teaching Library User Guide is designed to help you navigate the Teaching Library and deepen your understanding of how to use the Continuum as an assessment and planning tool. By following the suggestions for viewing and discussing the video segments, you will hone your ability to observe the behaviors of your readers and writers, and think about how your own teaching can support them in becoming increasingly proficient users of language and literacy.

Individual Study   **Small Group Study**   **Staff Developers**

You can use this Teaching Library for individual study, informal discussions with colleagues, or professional development seminars. However you use it, you will want to have your own copy of *The Continuum of Literacy Learning, Grades PreK–8* or *PreK–2* so that you can use it to plan for and guide your teaching on an ongoing basis. Specific suggestions for individuals, small groups, and staff developers are identified by these icons throughout the User Guide to help you customize your learning experience.

In addition to providing suggestions for viewing the teaching segments on each DVD, this guide also provides examples of how to use the Continuum to analyze texts, individual reading records, writing about reading samples, and examples of writing across the grades.

Where to Begin and the Sequence of Study

We recommend beginning your exploration of the Continuum and the Teaching Library with **DVD 1: Introduction and Assessment** to gain an overview of the entire Continuum, as well as a strong foundation in assessment. After working with DVD 1, continue your study by selecting an area of interest (e.g., Guided Reading; Writing; Phonics, Spelling, and Word Study; etc.) and turning to the corresponding section of the User Guide.

4 · Introduction
©2011 by Irene Fountas & Gay Su Pinnell

Each section of the User Guide begins with an introduction to the DVD and provides the following suggested sequence of study.

Research ▷ Here you will find a list of suggested background reading in other Fountas and Pinnell professional books to either get you started or help you revisit the frameworks and procedures for the particular instructional context. Though you will gain insight into these instructional frameworks and procedures by watching the video segments, the Teaching Library and User Guide are designed for in-depth thinking about the reading and writing behaviors to notice, teach, and support across the grades. They do not provide explicit information about how to initiate or conduct these types of lessons in your classroom. Therefore, it is helpful to familiarize yourself with procedures for the particular instructional context you are viewing by reading and/or by trying out a few lessons on your own.

Select a Clip and Print Supporting Materials ▷ This section provides a description of each teaching segment found on the DVD you have selected as well as a list of supporting materials available in the PDF Resources section. To customize your experience, select teaching segments that are close to the text levels or grade level(s) for which you are interested and print all necessary supporting materials.

Preview ▷ Before viewing the teaching segment(s) you select, watch the introduction to the DVD and preview the highlighted continuum. The preview section of the User Guide provides suggestions and guiding questions to help you think about the challenges for teaching and learning within the particular instructional context, and familiarizes you with aspects of the Continuum to enhance your viewing experience.

View Without Commentary ▷ After completing the preview, we recommend you choose to view the selected video clip **without commentary**. A set of guiding questions is offered in each section to focus your observations.

Think and/or Discuss ▷ After watching the video, take some time to think about your observations and discuss them with colleagues if you are working in a group.

Revisit the Continuum ▷ The next step will be to reopen the Continuum to the section you viewed earlier and identify some specific bullets that you can connect to the lesson you observed.

View With Commentary ▷ Following your review of the Continuum, you can play the video segment **with commentary** and compare what you have observed and discussed with the analysis offered on the DVD. Listening to the clips with commentary is particularly helpful for teachers working through the clips on their own as it provides another perspective in thinking about the reading and writing behaviors observed and taught.

Extend ▷ In each section, you will also find suggestions for extending your understanding of how to use the Continuum in your assessment and planning. You will have the opportunity to strengthen your understanding of what your readers and writers know and what you need to help them learn what to do next. For more ideas for extending your learning using *The Continuum of Literacy Learning*, you can download the *Study Guide for The Continuum of Literacy Learning: A Guide to Teaching* at http://www.heinemann.com/shared/studyGuides/E01001/studyGuide.pdf.

Give It a Try ▷ This section provides practical, easy-to-implement suggestions for how to get started using the Continuum to assess and plan for the particular instructional context highlighted on the DVD.

DVD 1

Introduction and Assessment

The first DVD in the Teaching Library provides an overview of the organization and content of *The Continuum of Literacy Learning, Grades PreK–8/PreK–2* as well as ideas for using the Teaching Library. It also offers an in-depth look at the value of systematic, standardized assessment of authentic reading, writing, and talking in the classroom. The Assessment section provides the opportunity to practice close observation by analyzing the reading behaviors of three individual readers as they process text. Being able to observe and analyze the reading and writing behaviors of students is fundamental to the planning of effective instruction. The work done in this section around assessment will impact the way you look at students across instructional contexts by sharpening your observational skills and will help you learn how to use the Continuum as an assessment tool.

Take a moment now to listen to the introductory material on DVD 1 as well as the segment on *The Values of Assessment*.

For the rest of the Assessment section, use the Guided Reading continuum, which is organized by text level. As with all of the reading continua in *The Continuum of Literacy Learning*, the Guided Reading continuum describes important behaviors for **thinking within, beyond, and about text**. These terms are briefly defined in the segment labeled *Analyzing Individual Reading Behaviors* on the DVD and described in more detail in the front matter of the Continuum. Inside the back cover of your Continuum, you'll also find a graphic representation of these systems of strategic actions with brief descriptions of each.

Now, listen to the segment on *Analyzing Individual Reading Behaviors* and take a moment to browse through the sections detailing the systems of strategic actions in *The Continuum of Literacy Learning, Grades PreK–8* or *PreK–2*.

To maximize your experience observing the three individual readers process text in the Assessment section, follow the suggested sequence of study that follows.

Research ▷

It is essential to understand how readers process written text with comprehension and fluency in order to support in their growth as readers. To help deepen your understanding of the systems of strategic actions, learn how to better observe your students' reading behaviors, and integrate formal and informal assessment into your reading workshop, you may want to read or revisit the following chapters and texts:

Teaching for Comprehending and Fluency, Fountas and Pinnell, Heinemann, 2006

- Chapter 1: "Understanding Readers, Texts, and Teaching"
- Chapter 2: "Helping Students Build a System for Processing a Variety of Texts"
- Chapter 3: "Reading Is Thinking: Within, Beyond, and About the Text"
- Chapter 4: "Helping Students Develop Systems of Strategic Actions to Sustain Processing"
- Chapter 5: "Helping Students Develop Systems of Strategic Actions for Expanding Thinking"
- Chapter 8: "Assessing Comprehension and Fluency to Document Progress and Inform Teaching"
- Chapter 9: "The Role of Talk, Writing, and Benchmark Books in Assessing Comprehension"

When Readers Struggle: Teaching That Works, Fountas and Pinnell, Heinemann, 2009

- Chapter 2: "Effective Readers: What Do They Do?"
- Chapter 3: "Going Off Track: Why and How?"
- Chapter 4: "Reading Behavior: What Does It Tell Us?"
- Chapter 5: "Change Over Time: Processing Systems in the Making"

Guided Reading: Good First Teaching for All Children, Fountas and Pinnell, Heinemann, 1996

- Chapter 6: "Using Assessment to Inform Teaching"
- Chapter 7: "Using Running Records"

Guiding Readers and Writers, Fountas and Pinnell, Heinemann, 2001

- Chapter 18: "Understanding the Reading Process"
- Chapter 28: "Making Teaching Decisions Using Continuous Assessment"

Select a Clip and Print Supporting Materials ▷

For this section, we suggest you watch all three video clips and notice the significant reading behaviors demonstrated by each individual reader. Supporting materials are available in the PDF Resources section of your DVD. Print any forms you plan to use by putting your DVD into a computer and clicking on the PDF Resources link.

Video Segment Descriptions and Running Times

Tarik reads *Socks*: Tarik reads the level C Benchmark Assessment System text *Socks.* You can create your own running record of this reading or follow along with a completed record to analyze this reader's behaviors. (12:49)

Richard reads *Our Teacher Mr. Brown*: Richard reads the level D Benchmark Assessment System text *Our Teacher Mr. Brown.* You can create your own running record of this reading or follow along with a completed record to analyze this reader's behaviors. (20:43)

Glory reads *Our New Neighbors*: Glory reads the level J Benchmark Assessment System text *Our New Neighbors*. You can create your own running record of this reading or follow along with a completed record to analyze this reader's behaviors (20:37).

PDF Resources

MATERIALS FOR VIEWING TEACHING SEGMENTS

Reading Record Recording Forms: Whether you are a staff developer, a member of a study group, or an individual, you may want to use these forms to view or record the reading behaviors of the readers in the clips.

- *Socks* Recording Form without coding
- *Socks* Recording Form with coding
- *Our Teacher Mr. Brown* Recording Form with coding
- *Our Teacher Mr. Brown* Recording Form without coding
- *Our New Neighbors* Recording Form with coding
- *Our New Neighbors* Recording Form without coding
- Coding and Scoring At a Glance

Text Analysis Forms: You will find printable copies of the text analyses included in the User Guide in this section. These may be useful to print if you are working with colleagues or a large group since they will not all have access to the User Guide.

- Text Analysis of *Socks*, level C
- Text Analysis of *Our Teacher Mr. Brown*, level D
- Text Analysis of *Our New Neighbors*, level J
- Text Analysis Form (optional)

MATERIALS FOR EXTENDING UNDERSTANDING
(See notes under Extend to decide whether you will need these materials)

- Randi's Reading Record (level F, *Anna's New Glasses*)
- Jakob's Reading Record (level F, *Anna's New Glasses*)
- Kulsum's Reading Record (level G, *Bubbles*)

Preview ▷

Turn to the Guided Reading continuum, level C, in your volume of *The Continuum of Literacy Learning*. You will notice the first part of the level C continuum begins with a general description of readers for whom this level will be just right for instruction. Though not all readers are the same, readers at this level should be able to process texts effectively with the characteristics described in this section. For more details about the *Selecting Texts* section, begin playing the Assessment clip on the DVD and pause when the authors suggest looking at these characteristics in more detail. During this time, you may want to follow the suggestions below for looking at the characteristics of text. In addition, you will find analyses for each text used on the DVD as well as suggestions for thinking about how these characteristics may impact the reader's processing.

Selecting Texts and Selecting Goals

In the first teaching clip, you will observe Tarik reading *Socks*, a level C text. This book is at his instructional level, which means it is slightly more challenging than a book he could read independently. However, he can still read it with 95% accuracy. As you see from the analysis of *Socks* in

Figure 1.1, not all books will have all of the features described in the *Selecting Texts* sections of the Continuum so you will always want to read and think about the characteristics of each particular text you choose to use with your students. It is also important to note that text characteristics are not inherently supportive or demanding. Depending on your reader's background and processing system, certain characteristics will be more challenging than others. It is not enough to look at the characteristics in isolation. Consider what behaviors and understandings your readers have in their control to think about how they might process a text.

Review the text analysis in Figure 1.1 and think about the following questions. If you have Fountas and Pinnell's *Benchmark Assessment System 1*, you may want to pull out the three texts featured in this section: *Socks, Our Teacher Mr. Brown,* and *Our New Neighbors.*

Individual Study

1. Think about students in your classroom who might be reading texts similar to *Socks.*

   - Which text characteristics described in Figure 1.1 will support their processing of this text?

   - Which will challenge them as they attempt to read with comprehension and fluency?

2. Compare your thinking to Figure 1.2, which lists what a typical reader at this level might find supportive or challenging when reading this text.

   - How will understanding the supports and challenges of a text inform your observation of students' reading behaviors as they process the text?

3. Now turn to the *Selecting Goals: Behaviors and Understandings to Notice, Teach, and Support* section for level C of the Guided Reading continuum. Scan the list of behaviors

organized into the larger categories of **thinking within, beyond, and about the text**. Within those categories, the behaviors and understandings are organized using the twelve systems of strategic actions.

   - Think again about a student you know reading at this level. What types of thinking would you expect to see as you observe this student reading? Which behaviors would you likely need to support or teach?

4. Repeat this process using Figures 1.3, 1.4, 1.5 and 1.6 for each individual reader on the DVD. The authors will prompt you on the DVD to complete this preview before watching each reader process the text.

Small Group Study & Staff Developers

1. In a small group(s), have each person think about a reader they know who can read books similar to *Socks.* Looking over the text characteristics in Figure 1.1, have them share with one another what characteristics they think would be supportive or challenging for their particular reader.

   - Observe and discuss how these supports and challenges are the same or different for the readers discussed.

   - How will understanding the supports and challenges of a text inform your observation of students' reading behaviors as they process the text?

2. Now turn to the *Selecting Goals: Behaviors and Understandings to Notice, Teach, and Support* section for level C of the Guided Reading continuum. Scan the list of behaviors organized into the larger categories of **thinking within, beyond, and about the text**. Within those categories, the behaviors and understandings are organized using the systems of strategic actions.

©2011 by Irene Fountas & Gay Su Pinnell

- Ask your colleagues to think again about students they know reading at this level and discuss:

  - What types of thinking would they expect to see as they observe this student reading?

- Which behaviors would they likely need to support or teach?

Text Analysis: *Socks* (Level C)
Using Guided Reading Continuum, Selecting Texts

Text Factor	Analysis
Genre and Form	■ Realistic Fiction ■ Form: Picture Book
Text Structure	■ Simple narrative with several repetitive episodes
Content	■ Familiar, easy content (family and pet cat named Socks) ■ All concepts supported by pictures
Themes and Ideas	■ Concrete, easy-to-understand idea (waking a sleeping cat) ■ Familiar theme
Language and Literary Features	■ Amusing, one-dimensional characters ■ Repeating, natural alternating language patterns ("Wake up, Socks!" I said. I said, "Wake up, Socks!") ■ Simple dialogue assigned by *said* ■ Told in first person
Sentence Complexity	■ Simple, predictable sentence structure but alternating patterns ■ Last sentence breaks from the repetition by adding the word *can* ■ Subject precedes verb and alternates with verb preceding subject ■ The phrase, "I said," alternates position in the sentence
Vocabulary	■ Vocabulary words familiar to children and likely to be used in their oral language ■ Word meanings illustrated by pictures ■ Some content words illustrated in the text (*chair, couch, window, bed, rug, door, table*)

Figure 1.1 Text Analysis: *Socks*

continues

Text Analysis: *Socks* (Level C)
Using Guided Reading Continuum, Selecting Texts

Text Factor	Analysis
Words	<ul><li>Mostly one-syllable words except for *sleeping, window,* and *table*</li><li>Greater range of high-frequency words (*up, said, the, was, she, on, my, by, can*)</li><li>Some words with -*s* and -*ing* (*Socks, sleeping*)</li><li>Some words used in different language structure ("'Wake up,' I said," and "'I said, 'Wake up.'")</li><li>Words with easy spelling patterns (*wake, bed, rug*)</li></ul>
Illustrations	<ul><li>Illustrations that match print very closely</li><li>Meaning carried in the text but closely supported by the illustrations on every page</li><li>Consistent layout of illustrations and print (print on left and illustrations on right)</li><li>Very simple illustrations with little distracting detail</li></ul>
Book and Print Features	**Length:** <ul><li>16 pages (eight pages of print)</li><li>Consistent four lines of print per page</li></ul>**Print and Layout:** <ul><li>Large, plain text</li><li>Ample spacing between words and lines</li><li>Print clearly separated by pictures</li><li>Consistent placement of print</li><li>Line breaks match ends of phrases</li></ul>**Punctuation:** <ul><li>Periods</li><li>Commas</li><li>Exclamation marks</li><li>Quotation marks</li></ul>**Tools:** <ul><li>Speech bubble on last page (*Purr*)</li></ul>

Figure 1.1   Text Analysis: *Socks (continued)*

Text Analysis: *Socks* **(Level C)**

Potential Supports and Challenges

Supports	■ Familiar content and theme (waking a sleeping cat)
	■ Simple, predictable oral language patterns
	■ Large print with ample spacing
	■ Meaning carried in the text but closely supported by the illustrations on every page
Challenges	■ The phrase, "I said," alternates position in the sentences
	■ Some sentences do not begin with high-frequency words
	■ Changes in prepositional phrases (*on, by, under*)
	■ Change in sentence pattern on the last page with addition of high-frequency word *can*

Figure 1.2   Potential Supports and Challenges: *Socks*

Text Analysis: *Our Teacher Mr. Brown* (Level D)
Using Guided Reading Continuum, Selecting Texts

Text Factor	Analysis
Genre and Form	■ Simple informational text ■ Form: Picture Book
Text Structure	■ Focused on one simple topic (an excellent teacher)
Content	■ Familiar, easy content (activities in school) ■ Most concepts supported by pictures
Themes and Ideas	■ Familiar theme and ideas (a boy tells about his special teacher)
Language and Literary Features	■ Engaging, one-dimensional characters (Carl and Mr. Brown) ■ More complex repeating language patterns ("Mr. Brown helps us read books. We like to read books. Mr. Brown plays games with us. We like to play ball.") ■ Greater variety of language structures (alternates between "Mr. Brown..." and "We like to...") ■ Text with familiar settings close to children's experience (school) ■ Simple dialogue assigned to speaker ■ Simple sequence of events (the activities Mr. Brown does with the children in Carl's class)
Sentence Complexity	■ One longer sentence with eight words ("We like to read the stories to him.") ■ Many sentences with prepositional phrases ■ Mostly simple sentences (subject and predicate)
Vocabulary	■ Almost all vocabulary familiar to children and likely to be used in their oral language ■ Word meanings illustrated by pictures (*read, paint, draw, play, write*)

Figure 1.3   Text Analysis: *Our Teacher Mr. Brown*

continues

Text Analysis: *Our Teacher Mr. Brown* **(Level D)**	
Using Guided Reading Continuum, Selecting Texts	

Text Factor	Analysis
Words	■ All one- to two-syllable words ■ Mostly simple plurals (except for *stories)* ■ Many high-frequency words ■ Some words with -*s* (*books, games, pictures)* and apostrophe -*s* (*teacher's)* ■ Many words with easy, predictable letter-sound relationships ■ Mostly simple spelling patterns
Illustrations	■ Highly supportive illustrations (photographs) that generally match the text ■ Illustrations consistently on right-hand page until pages 14, 15, 16 ■ More details in the illustrations
Book and Print Features	Length: ■ Very short, nine pages of print ■ Mostly two to six lines of print per page (but variable) Print and Layout: ■ Ample space between words and lines ■ Print in large plain font ■ Some sentences that wrap over two lines ■ Sentences beginning on the left in most of the text ■ Print clearly separated from pictures in most of the text ■ Line breaks match ends of phrases and sentences Punctuation: ■ Periods ■ Apostrophes ■ Exclamation points Tools: ■ Two different photographs on page 15 to match two different school activities ("We like to write stories." and "We like to play ball.")

Figure 1.3 Text Analysis: *Our Teacher Mr. Brown (continued)*

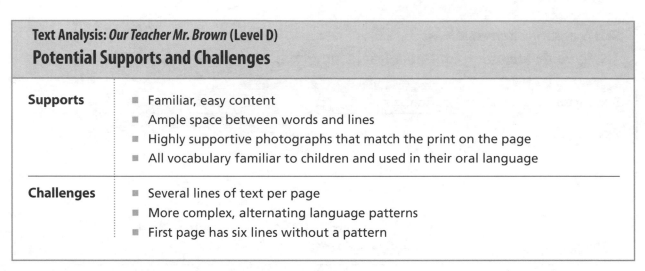

Text Analysis: *Our Teacher Mr. Brown* **(Level D)**
Potential Supports and Challenges

Supports	■ Familiar, easy content
	■ Ample space between words and lines
	■ Highly supportive photographs that match the print on the page
	■ All vocabulary familiar to children and used in their oral language
Challenges	■ Several lines of text per page
	■ More complex, alternating language patterns
	■ First page has six lines without a pattern

Figure 1.4   Potential Supports and Challenges: *Our Teacher Mr. Brown*

Text Analysis: *Our New Neighbors* **(Level J)**
Using Guided Reading Continuum, Selecting Texts

Text Factor	Analysis
Genre and Form	■ Realistic Fiction (simple mystery) ■ Form: Picture Book
Text Structure	■ Narrative with more elaborated episodes
Content	■ Familiar content (invitation to meet the new neighbors and their horses)
Themes and Ideas	■ Light, humorous story typical of childhood experiences ■ Theme accessible given typical experiences of children (having new neighbors)
Language and Literary Features	■ Amusing or engaging characters, some of whom have more than one dimension ■ Variety of dialogue between more than two characters (dialogue between new neighbors, Flo and Max, and all of the neighbors) ■ Multiple episodes taking place across time (neighbors making predictions about the mystery of the horses)

Figure 1.5   Text Analysis: *Our New Neighbors*

continues

Text Analysis: *Our New Neighbors* (Level J)
Using Guided Reading Continuum, Selecting Texts

Text Factor	Analysis
Sentence Complexity	■ Many longer (more than ten words), more complex sentences (prepositional phrases, introductory clauses, lists of nouns) ■ Sentences with embedded clauses and phrases ("Every day when I pass that house, I hear loud noises, like someone is hammering.") ■ Variation in placement of subject, verb, adjectives, and adverbs ■ Many compound sentences
Vocabulary	■ Most vocabulary words known by children through oral language or reading ■ Content words illustrated with pictures (*sign, merry-go-round, neighbors, barn*) ■ Wide variety of words to assign dialogue (*said, called, asked, cried, added, piped up, grinned*)
Words	■ Many two-syllable words and a few three-syllable words (*surprise, around, everyone, hammering, neighbors, wondering*) ■ Plurals and contractions (*horses, they're, they'll, there's, don't, it's*) ■ Wide range of high-frequency words ■ Many words with inflectional endings (*leaned, grinned, turned, hammering, wondering, popped, fixing*, etc.) ■ Some words with complex letter-sound relationships (*mystery, neighbors, noises*) ■ Some complex spelling patterns (*neighbors, ponies, hammering*) ■ Multisyllable words that are generally easy to take apart or decode (*began, someone, something, corner*) ■ Some easy compound words (*birthday, maybe*)
Illustrations	■ Some illustrations complex with many ideas (thought bubbles) ■ Some complex and artistic illustrations that communicate meaning to match or extend the text ■ Illustrations that support interpretation, enhance enjoyment, set mood but are not necessary for understanding

continues

Figure 1.5   Text Analysis: *Our New Neighbors (continued)*

Text Analysis: *Our New Neighbors* (Level J)
Using Guided Reading Continuum, Selecting Texts

Text Factor	Analysis
Book and Print Features	**Length:** ■ 16 pages ■ Many lines of print on a page (from 1 to 10 lines) **Print and Layout:** ■ Ample space between lines ■ Some text in smaller font size (notes from neighbors) ■ Words in bold that are important to meaning (notes from neighbors) ■ Sentences carrying over two to three lines ■ Some sentences starting in middle of a line ■ Print clearly separated from pictures ■ Variety in layout but illustrations mostly below the print **Punctuation:** ■ Periods ■ Commas ■ Quotations marks ■ Exclamation points ■ Question marks ■ Dashes **Tools:** ■ Invitation and notes from neighbor embedded in the illustrations

Figure 1.5   Text Analysis: *Our New Neighbors (continued)*

Text Analysis: *Our New Neighbors* (Level J)
Potential Supports and Challenges

Supports	▪ Engaging story with simple mystery ▪ Light, humorous story typical of some children's experiences ▪ Most vocabulary words known by children through oral language or reading
Challenges	▪ Many lines of print on a page ▪ Sentences wrapping over two to three lines ▪ Some sentences starting middle of a line

Figure 1.6 Potential Supports and Challenges: *Our New Neighbors*

View Without Commentary ▷

After completing the preview of the Continuum, press play and view the clip of the students reading **without commentary**. Remember you may choose to complete the coding of the reading record using the blank recording form or follow along using the completed reading record. Both are printable from DVD 1 under PDF Resources. You may also want to print *Coding and Scoring At a Glance* also found in PDF Resources if you need to familiarize yourself with the coding symbols used in these reading records.

Note: Although this section of the DVD utilizes *Fountas and Pinnell Benchmark Assessment System* as a tool for the close observation of readers, you do not have to be using Benchmark Assessment with your students to use this portion of the DVD. The focus of this section of the DVD and User Guide is not to familiarize you with Benchmark Assessment but to give you an opportunity to observe the reading behaviors of students using *The Continuum of Literacy Learning*. The process of analyzing reading behaviors using the Continuum can translate to other formal and informal assessment systems, particularly to the use of running records.

While watching the video clip, make note of any reading behaviors you notice as evidence of the students' processing. Knowing that readers engage all of the strategic actions simultaneously and flexibly in their head as they construct the meaning of a text, you will want to look for evidence of these strategic actions as they read and talk about the text. As you watch, also pay attention to the way the reader negotiates the characteristics of texts you observed in the preview section.

Think and/or Discuss ▷

 Individual Study

Pause the video segment before watching it with commentary. Review your notes and think about the evidence of specific behaviors and understandings you saw as the student read and discussed the text. You may want to use the *Guide for Observing and Noting Reading Behaviors* found in PDF Resources to focus your thinking.

 Small Group Study & Staff Developers

Have partners work together to think about and discuss the evidence of specific behaviors and understandings by the reader in the clip. Discuss the following questions:

- What strategic actions were being used by the reader as the reader processed the text?

- What strategic actions will the teacher need to support or teach for?

Revisit the Continuum ▷

 Individual, Small Group & Staff Developers

After you have done some thinking on your own, reopen the Continuum to the section you viewed earlier. You may want to use the form *Analyzing Reading Behaviors* found in PDF Resources on the DVD to help guide and record your thinking.

- Identify the specific behaviors and understandings you saw demonstrated by the reader.

- Think about two or three bulleted behaviors you would want to teach for or support.

View With Commentary ▷

Now, play the video segment **with commentary** and compare what you have observed and discussed with the analysis on the DVD.

 Individual Study

Think about beginning a reflection journal in which you can record what you have learned from each section of the DVD.

- How will what you learned in this section impact your teaching? What do you want to work on in your teaching?

 Small Group Study & Staff Developers

After viewing the clip with commentary, have colleagues discuss the following:

- What have you learned from your observations and discussion that will help you in your teaching?

Extend ▷

Selecting Texts: Analyzing Text Characteristics

 Individual, Small Group & Staff Developers

If you have *Benchmark Assessment System 1*, you may want to deepen your understanding of text analysis by completing one of these text analyses on your own using the books *Socks, Our Teacher Mr. Brown,* and *Our New Neighbors* from the *Benchmark* System. You will find a blank Text Analysis form available on the DVD for this purpose. After you complete the text analysis either on your own or with a colleague, compare it to the analyses in Figures 1.1, 1.3, and 1.5.

Note: It is not realistic to think you can complete an in-depth text analysis for every text you use with your students; however, taking the time to explore the characteristics of texts using *The Continuum of Literacy Learning* helps you hone your ability to look at texts for their potential supports and challenges. Understanding the supports and demands of a text not only facilitates your observation of readers but also greatly impacts your planning and instruction. We discuss the instructional implications of this work in more depth in the Interactive Read-Aloud and Literature Discussion and Guided Reading sections of the User Guide.

Selecting Goals: Analyzing Behaviors and Understandings Evidenced in Reading Records

Analyzing reading behaviors to identify what your readers are able to do, what they need to learn how to do, or what they need to learn to do *more consistently* allows you to be specific with your instruction. As you may have noticed from your work with the DVD so far, the Guided Reading continuum can be used as a tool for both assessment and instruction. To further hone your ability to use the Continuum in this way, you may want to print out the additional reading records available on the DVD under **PDF Resources: Materials for Extension Activities**.

 Individual, Small Group & Staff Developers

After printing these records, turn to the appropriate text level in the Guided Reading continuum and complete an analysis of the reading behaviors in the reading record. Think about the following questions:

- What behaviors and understandings does this reader control? What is your evidence?

- What are some behaviors and understandings that you might focus on next in your instruction?

 Small Group Study & Staff Developers

Ask participants in the group to discuss their findings with one another.

 Individual, Small Group & Staff Developers

Compare your findings with the analyses below.

- How did the Guided Reading continuum help you notice the behaviors and understandings evidenced by this reader?

- How will the Continuum help you connect assessment with specific instruction?

Analyses of Reading Records

Let's first look at Randi's reading of a fictional text, *Anna's New Glasses,* level F (Figure 1.7). It is important to note that this record provides just one glimpse of this reader and is in no way comprehensive. Randi's teacher would want to take more than one assessment into account when thinking about what Randi is able to do as a reader and future directions for Randi's learning.

Figure 1.7a — *Anna's New Glasses* • LEVEL F • FICTION — Recording Form

Student: Randi   Grade: _____   Date: _____
Teacher: _____   School: _____

Recording Form

Part One: Oral Reading

Place the book in front of the student. Read the title and introduction.

Introduction: Anna was getting ready for school. Her mom said she might need to get glasses to see better. But Anna didn't want glasses. Read to find out what happened when she got her new glasses.

Anna's New Glasses Level F, RW: 220

Page	Text
2	"I am ready for school," said Anna. She had a new red backpack and new shoes. "We have one more thing to do," said her mom. "You may need to get some glasses."
4	"I don't need glasses!" said Anna. "You may need glasses to help you read," said her mom.

Subtotal: 28 4 4 9 6 6 3

Figure 1.7b — Recording Form — *Anna's New Glasses* • LEVEL F • FICTION

Part One: Oral Reading *continued*

Page	Text
4 cont.	"Do you want to read at school?"
5	"I want to read," said Anna. "I love books! But I don't want glasses."
6	Anna went to the doctor. "You **do** need glasses," said the doctor.
7	Anna looked at the glasses.
8	"I don't like these glasses," she said.

Subtotal: 7 1 4 4 3 0 0 1

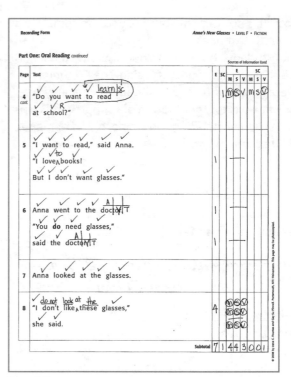

Figure 1.7c — *Anna's New Glasses* • LEVEL F • FICTION — Recording Form

Part One: Oral Reading *continued*

Page	Text
9	"Look at the purple glasses," said Mom. Anna put on the purple glasses.
11	Anna put on some red glasses. "I like red and I like these red glasses," she said. "You look great in those glasses," said Mom.
12	It was the first day of school.

Subtotal: 50 2 2 4 0 0 0

Figure 1.7d — Recording Form — *Anna's New Glasses* • LEVEL F • FICTION

Part One: Oral Reading *continued*

Page	Text
12 cont.	Anna put her new red glasses in her new red backpack.
13	"Don't forget your glasses," said Mom. "I put them in my backpack," said Anna. "Put your glasses on at school," said Mom.
15	Anna and her mom walked to school.

Subtotal: 30 2 2 3 0 0 0

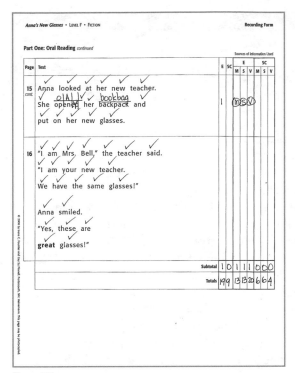

Figure 1.7e

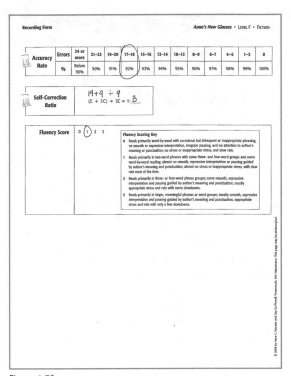

Figure 1.7f

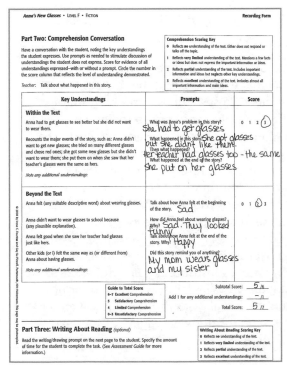

Figure 1.7g

RANDI	
Observations of Behaviors and Understandings (Guided Reading Continuum, Level F)	**Analysis of Behavioral Evidence**
Solving Words ■ Recognize 50 or more high-frequency words within continuous text automatically ■ Use language structure, meaning, and visual information in a coordinated way to solve words	Randi seems to recognize several high-frequency words (e.g. *you, it, of, was, the, day, said*). However, Randi's lack of fluency may be related to how quickly he recognizes these words. If this is the case, his teacher may want to work on his ability to retrieve these words more quickly by working with high-frequency words during word work in guided reading. Randi's use of multiple sources of information to solve words is evident in his self-corrections. For example, he self-corrects *ready* for *red* in the first line of reading. He is obviously using visual information when he says "red." However, as he listens to the language structure and realizes that *red* does not sound right or make sense, he solves the word and changes it to *ready*. He does the same with *new* for *need* later in his reading.
Monitoring and Correcting ■ Reread a phrase to problem-solve, self-correct, or confirm ■ Use meaning, language structure, and visual information to self-monitor or self-correct reading ■ Use known words to self-monitor and correct	Randi often rereads to self-correct. For example, on page 4 of the text, he realizes that "I don't *new* glasses!" doesn't sound right or make sense. He goes back to the beginning of the sentence and rereads, self-correcting *need* for *new*. His self-corrections throughout the reading demonstrate his use of multiple sources of information (e.g., "You may need glasses to *here* you read," said her mom). Randi self-corrects with the word *help* realizing that *here* doesn't sound right or make sense. He obviously is also paying attention to visual information, substituting *help* with a word that looks very similar. This self-monitoring occurs in several cases throughout the record (e.g., *thing* for *think* on page 2 of the text, *read* for *learn* on page 4). The number of times

Figure 1.8 Observations of Behaviors and Understandings: *Randi*

continues

RANDI	
Observations of Behaviors and Understandings (Guided Reading Continuum, Level F)	**Analysis of Behavioral Evidence**
Monitoring and Correcting, cont.	Randi stops and asks his teacher for an unknown word also demonstrates that Randi is monitoring his reading. He clearly knows when his reading has broken down even when he is unsure of how to deal with it.
Searching for and Using Information ■ Reread to search for and use information or confirm reading ■ Use all sources of information together to solve words while reading (sometimes) ■ Process texts with simple dialogue and some pronouns, all assigned to speakers ■ Notice, search for, remember, and discuss information that is important to understanding	As described above, we see evidence that Randi is searching for and using multiple sources of information to solve words, monitor, and self-correct his reading. We can tell from the comprehension conversation at the end of the record that he is able to remember and discuss information that is important for understanding the story. For example, he is able to recount that Anna had to get glasses and that she did not like them. He also remembered that Anna's teacher had the same glasses and that at the end, Anna puts on her glasses.
Summarizing ■ Notice a series of events in order to link them ■ Understand a simple sequence of events ■ Provide an oral summary with appropriate details in sequence ■ Remember important information	As noted above, Randi is able to recount the series of events in the story and summarize important information and appropriate details in sequence when discussing the text.
Making Connections ■ Make and discuss connections between texts and reader's personal experiences	Randi makes a personal connection about his mom and sister both wearing glasses like Anna in the story.
Inferring ■ Infer and discuss characters' feelings, motives, and attributes	Randi is able to infer that Anna feels happy at the end of the story; however, it is unclear if he connects this to the fact that her teacher had the same glasses.

Figure 1.8 Observations of Behaviors and Understandings: *Randi*

RANDI	
Behaviors and Understandings to Teach and Support (Guided Reading Continuum, Level F)	**Instructional Implications**
Solving Words ■ Remove the ending from base words to solve new words ■ Use letter-sound analysis from left to right to read a new word ■ Use sounds related to vowels to solve words ■ Take apart many easy new words "on the run" while reading for meaning ■ Take apart compound words	Randi needs more instruction on how to solve unknown words. Randi's strong self-monitoring skills alert him when he doesn't know a word or if what he said did not make sense, but he often asks the teacher what the word is instead of attempting to solve the word himself. We see this particularly with two-syllable words (e.g., *purple, doctor*). He would benefit from learning how to break apart two-syllable words and use letter-sound analysis from left to right to read a new word. Lastly, he needs more instruction on how to remove the endings of a base word to solve a word (e.g., *walk—ed*; and *open—ed*). Randi's teacher may decide to work on these word-solving strategies during word work in guided reading or during word study.
Maintaining Fluency ■ Demonstrate phrased, fluent oral reading ■ Reflect language syntax and meaning through phrasing and expression ■ Reflect punctuation through appropriate pausing and intonation while reading orally	According to his fluency score, Randi is reading primarily in two-word phrases with almost no expressive interpretation. Randi would benefit from instruction in reading in meaningful phrased groups. He is able to monitor his reading for meaning so he should be able to learn how to reflect the meaning and syntax through phrasing and expression. After focusing on his phrasing, his teacher may also want to work with him on how to read the punctuation the author has written with appropriate pausing and intonation.
Making Connections ■ Make and discuss connections between texts and reader's personal experiences ■ Make connections between the text and other texts that have been read or heard	Randi does make a personal connection to the text when he talks about his mom and sister both having glasses, but he seems ready to learn how to make deeper connections to a text. His teacher will want to work with him on connecting to the

Figure 1.9   Behaviors and Understandings to Teach and Support: *Randi*

continues

RANDI	
Behaviors and Understandings to Teach and Support (Guided Reading Continuum, Level F)	**Instructional Implications**
Making Connections, *cont*.	feelings in a book or to the theme of the book. Interactive read-aloud provides an excellent opportunity for students to begin to learn how to make deeper personal connections to text. By using text sets grouped around similar themes, his teacher will support him in also learning how to make connections between texts.
Inferring ■ Interpret causes for feelings, motives, or actions	As described above, Randi is able to infer that Anna is happy from the text. However, it is unclear whether he connects her happiness to the fact that her teacher has the same glasses. He might have understood this to be the cause for her feelings and just did not communicate it during the comprehension conversation. His teacher will want to watch his ability to interpret the cause of a character's feelings in future reading and determine whether he needs further support in this area.

Figure 1.9 Behaviors and Understandings to Teach and Support: *Randi (continued)*

Summary of Instructional Implications

Randi's teacher will want to pick two or three of these behaviors and understandings to focus on in her teaching. Randi seems to need the most support in learning more efficient word-solving strategies, which might be accomplished during shared reading, word study, or word work in his guided reading lessons as well as in his reading of the text. He would also benefit from learning how to read with phrasing and expression. His teacher may want to provide him with more opportunities for shared and performance reading to give him additional opportunities to read aloud and work on his ability to read fluently.

Let's take a look at another reader's processing of the same text. Using the Guided Reading continuum, level F once again, we will analyze Jakob's reading of *Anna's New Glasses* (Figure 1.10).

Figure 1.10a (top left)

Anna's New Glasses • LEVEL F • FICTION Recording Form

Student: Jakob Grade _____ Date _____
Teacher _____ School _____

Recording Form
Part One: Oral Reading

Place the book in front of the student. Read the title and introduction.

Introduction: Anna was getting ready for school. Her mom said she might need to get glasses to see better. But Anna didn't want glasses. Read to find out what happened when she got her new glasses.

Page	Text (Anna's New Glasses Level F, RW: 220)	E	SC	E (M S V)	SC (M S V)
2	"I am ready for school," said Anna. / She had a new red backpack / and new shoes. / "We have one more thing to / do," said her mom. "You may / need to get some glasses."	2 / 1 / 1 / 1		M S V / M S V	
4	"I don't need glasses!" / said Anna. / "You may need glasses to help / you read," said her mom.	1 / 1		M S V / M S V M S V	
	Subtotal	6 1		3 4 6	1 0 0

Figure 1.10a Jakob's Reading Record

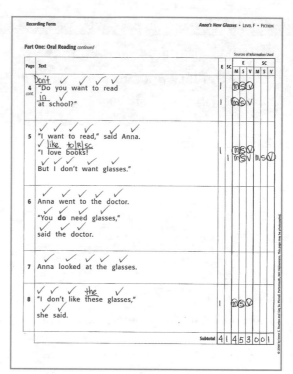

Figure 1.10b (top right)

Recording Form   *Anna's New Glasses* • LEVEL F • FICTION

Part One: Oral Reading *continued*

Page	Text	E	SC	E (M S V)	SC (M S V)
4 cont.	"Do you want to read / in / at school?"	1 / 1		M S V / M S V	
5	"I want to read," said Anna. / "I love books! / But I don't want glasses."	1	1	M S V / M S V	M S V
6	Anna went to the doctor. / "You **do** need glasses," / said the doctor.				
7	Anna looked at the glasses.				
8	"I don't like these glasses," / she said.	1		M S V	
	Subtotal	4 1		4 5 3	0 0 1

Figure 1.10b

Figure 1.10c (bottom left)

Anna's New Glasses • LEVEL F • FICTION   Recording Form

Part One: Oral Reading *continued*

Page	Text	E	SC	E (M S V)	SC (M S V)
9	"Look at the purple glasses," / said Mom. / Anna put on / the purple glasses.	1 / 2		M S V / M S V	
11	Anna put on some red glasses. / "I like red and I like / these red glasses," she said. / "You look great in those / glasses," said Mom.	1 / 1 / 2		M S V / M S V / M S V M S V	
12	It was the first day / of school.				
	Subtotal	7 0		5 6 4	0 0 0

Figure 1.10c

Figure 1.10d (bottom right)

Recording Form   *Anna's New Glasses* • LEVEL F • FICTION

Part One: Oral Reading *continued*

Page	Text	E	SC	E (M S V)	SC (M S V)
12 cont.	Anna put her / new red glasses in / her new red backpack.				
13	"Don't forget your glasses," / said Mom. / "I put them in my backpack," / said Anna. / "Put your glasses on at school," / said Mom.	3		M S V	
15	Anna and her mom walked / to school.				
	Subtotal	3 0		1 1 0	0 0 0

Figure 1.10d

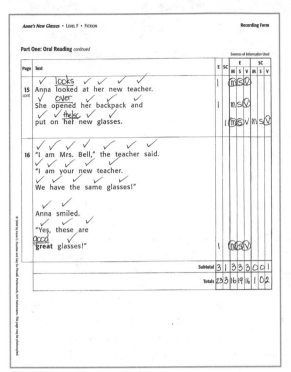

Figure 1.10e

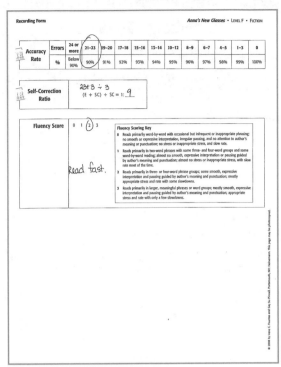

Figure 1.10f

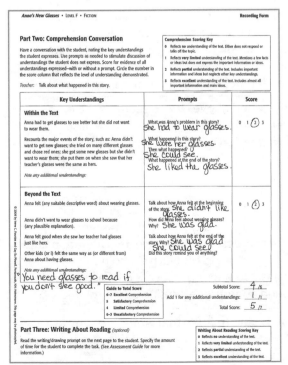

Figure 1.10g

JAKOB	
Observations of Behaviors and Understandings (Guided Reading Continuum, Level F)	**Analysis of Behavioral Evidence**
Solving Words ■ Recognize most words quickly ■ Recognize 50 or more high-frequency words within continuous text automatically	Jakob seems to recognize most words quickly, which enables him to read fast. However, his rapid reading in turn causes him to make several errors in accuracy. Despite some of his errors, he seems to recognize several high-frequency words (*we, said, am, some, you*, etc.).
Monitoring and Correcting ■ Use meaning, language structure, and visual information to self-monitor or self-correct reading (sometimes)	Jakob self-corrects a few times throughout the story based on information from multiple sources. For example, on page 4 of the text, he self-corrects *help* because *hear* doesn't make sense. His substitutions are also often meaningful, fit the structure of language and even look similar to the word (e.g., he substitutes *picked up* for *put on* on page 9). In these cases, he doesn't stop to confirm or self-correct since meaning has not broken down. However, there are cases where he substitutes words that do not sound right or make sense (see page 2) and he does not go back and self-correct. He would benefit from instruction in learning how to slow down, reread, and monitor more consistently.
Searching for and Using Information ■ Use all sources of information together to solve words while reading (sometimes) ■ Process texts with simple dialogue and some pronouns, all assigned to speakers	As described above, Jakob seems to have some understanding of how to use multiple sources of information while reading but does not use these strategic actions consistently.
Maintaining Fluency ■ Demonstrate phrased, fluent oral reading (somewhat) ■ Reflect some language syntax and meaning through phrasing and expression	According to Jakob's fluency score, he reads primarily in three and four-word phrases and demonstrates some expressive interpretation and pausing. However, his teacher also notes that he read fast, perhaps not reflecting punctuation through appropriate pausing and intonation.
Inferring ■ Infer and discuss characters' feelings, motives, and attributes	Jakob is able to infer that Anna is happy at the end, but does not appear to link these feelings to a cause.

Figure 1.11 Observations of Behaviors and Understandings: *Jakob*

JAKOB	
Behaviors and Understandings to Teach and Support (Guided Reading Continuum, Level F)	**Instructional Implications**
Monitoring and Correcting ■ Reread a phrase to problem-solve, self-correct, or confirm ■ Use meaning, language structure, and visual information to self-monitor and self-correct reading	Out of 23 errors, Jakob only self-corrects three times. Though he sometimes appears to use multiple sources of information to solve words or make meaningful substitutions, he would benefit from continued support in attending to whether something looks right, sounds right, and makes sense. He also needs to learn how to stop and reread in order to confirm his reading. He often is reading so fast that he does not bother to go back and make sure his reading makes sense. (For example on page 2 he reads, "You *my new* to get some glasses" instead of "You *may need* to get some glasses.") Had Jakob stopped and reread the phrase, he would have easily been able to correct his error. He is able to read the word *need* accurately just a few lines later.
Searching for and Using Information ■ Reread to search for and use information or confirm reading ■ Notice, search for, remember, and discuss information that is important to understanding	Jakob is unable to recall some of the significant events in the story (e.g., he does not mention that Anna's teacher put on the same glasses as Anna). He would benefit from instruction in how to find and recall important information from a text. This skill could be supported in guided reading.
Summarizing ■ Remember information to help in understanding the end of a story ■ Notice a series of events in order to link them ■ Provide an oral summary with appropriate details in sequence ■ Remember important information	As we can see from the comprehension conversation, Jakob is not able to summarize the most important points of the story. He appears to need more modeling in how to summarize a story and remember important information. If he slows down his reading, he may be able to focus more on the events in the story. His teacher could begin by modeling how to summarize the important information in a story during interactive read-aloud and in writing about reading.

Figure 1.12 Behaviors and Understandings to Teach and Support: *Jakob*

continues

JAKOB	
Behaviors and Understandings to Teach and Support (Guided Reading Continuum, Level F)	**Instructional Implications**
Maintaining Fluency ■ Reflect punctuation through appropriate pausing and intonation while reading orally	As Jakob adjusts his rate, he might be able to pay closer attention to the author's use of punctuation. Jakob would benefit from shared reading and guided reading in which his teacher demonstrates how to reflect punctuation through pausing and intonation.
Adjusting ■ Slow down or repeat to think about the meaning of the text and resume normal speed ■ Reread to solve words or think about ideas and resume good rate of reading	As his teacher notes, he read this story very fast, which impacts his ability to monitor his reading and to understand the story. By learning how to reread and slow down, Jakob will be able to monitor and correct and ultimately improve his comprehension.
Inferring ■ Interpret causes for feelings, motives, or actions	Jakob is able to infer that Anna is glad at the end of the story. However, he is unable to interpret the cause for her feelings, saying she is glad because she can see. He does not connect any of these emotions to the fact that her teacher has the same glasses. His teacher will want to support him in thinking about why characters feel the way they do during interactive read-aloud and guided reading.

Figure 1.12 Behaviors and Understandings to Teach and Support: *Jakob*

Summary of Instructional Implications

Jakob's teacher could take Jakob's instruction in many different directions to expand his ability to think within, beyond, and about the text. Jakob seems like he would benefit the most from learning to adjust his reading rate and slow down to begin to monitor and correct his reading. Learning to reread when his reading doesn't make sense will also help him search for and use the information in the text. Shared and performance reading would provide an authentic reason for Jakob to read aloud and begin noticing how to slow down his reading and reflect the author's meaning through his expression, paus-

ing, and intonation. As he adjusts his reading rate, he may find he is able to remember parts of the story in more detail. However, he will need further instruction in how to search for information in the text and remember important details sequentially to summarize his reading and understand it more fully. During interactive read-aloud and guided reading, his teacher will want to give Jakob opportunities to search for and recall information from the text to help him build his ability to summarize and notice the details of a story.

Let's now look at Kulsum's reading of a nonfiction text, *Bubbles,* level G (Figure 1.13).

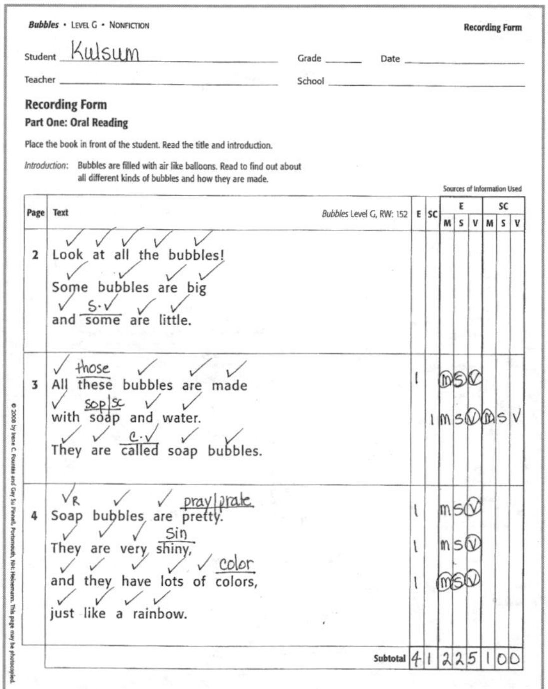

Figure 1.13a   Kulsum's Reading Record

Figure 1.13b

Figure 1.13c

Figure 1.13d

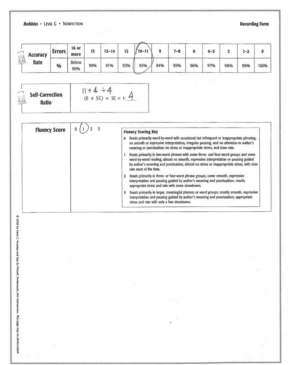

Figure 1.13e

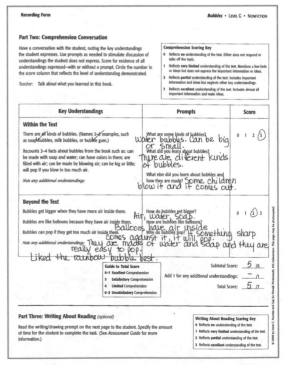

Figure 1.13f

KULSUM	
Observations of Behaviors and Understandings (Guided Reading Continuum, Level G)	**Analysis of Behavioral Evidence**
Solving Words ■ Quickly and automatically recognize 75 or more high-frequency words within continuous text ■ Use consonant and vowel letter-sound relationships to solve words ■ Use letter clusters (blends and digraphs) to solve words ■ Connect words that mean the same or almost the same to derive meaning from the text	Kulsum already knows a lot about word-solving. She makes meaningful substitutions most of the time and is able to solve words using multiple sources of information as we see from her solving of *straw* on page 10. She uses what she knows about clusters to make an approximation and then thinks about what would make sense to solve the word correctly. However, she needs to apply this knowledge of clusters more consistently. Kulsum also recognizes many high-frequency words (e.g., *some, are, big, look, and, all*). Kulsum does appear to use the consonant letter-sound relationship to solve some words; however, she appears to rely heavily on the first consonant of words and does not always read the whole word to solve it (e.g., *bubbles* for *balloons*). Kulsum also appears to connect words that mean almost the same to derive meaning from the text. For example, instead of saying *"blowing* air," she says *"bubbling* air" throughout the story. We can see from the comprehension conversation that she understood that air is blown inside of bubbles to form them.
Monitoring and Correcting ■ Use meaning, language structure, and visual information to monitor or self-correct reading	Though she needs to learn to do it more consistently, Kulsum demonstrates her use of meaning, language structure, and visual information in some of her self-corrections. (She corrects *soap* on page 3 because it doesn't make sense. Her close substitution of the word *sop* shows that she is using some visual information. In the same way, she says *stray* for *straw* and self-corrects based on meaning on page 10.)

Figure 1.14 Observations of Behaviors and Understandings: *Kulsum*

continues

KULSUM	
Observations of Behaviors and Understandings (Guided Reading Continuum, Level G)	**Analysis of Behavioral Evidence**
Searching for and Using Information ■ Use all sources of information together to solve words while reading (sometimes) ■ Notice, search for, remember, and discuss information that is important to understanding	Kulsum demonstrates her ability to remember and discuss important information during the comprehension conversation. She understands that there are different kinds and sizes of bubbles and that they are filled with air.
Summarizing ■ Remember the important information from a factual text	See evidence under Searching for and Using Information.
Synthesizing ■ Relate the content of the text to what is already known	In the comprehension conversation, Kulsum relates what she has learned about bubbles to what she knows about balloons. She explains both are filled with air and can be popped by sharp objects.

Figure 1.14 Observations of Behaviors and Understandings: *Kulsum (continued)*

KULSUM	
Behaviors and Understandings to Teach and Support (Guided Reading Continuum, Level G)	**Instructional Implications**
Solving Words ■ Use letter clusters (blends and digraphs) to solve words ■ Use left to right letter-sound analysis to read a word ■ Use known words and word parts (including onsets and rimes) to solve unknown words	Kulsum needs to learn how to apply her knowledge of clusters more consistently as evidenced by her substitutions of *bubbles* for *blowing* and *sin* for *shiny*. She would probably benefit from some quick word work around clusters in word work in guided reading, as well as while she reads the text. She also needs to learn to read the whole word. She is often only using the initial consonant when reading a word and frequently leaves off the ending (e.g., *bubbles* for *balloons* on page 6; *bubbling* for *blowing*; *girl* for *girl's* on page 10; *color* for *colors* on page 4). We know that she can read the word *blows* on page 14 but does not connect that to the word *blowing*. She would benefit from some work around using known words and word parts to solve unknown words as she reads text and during word work at the end of guided reading. Lastly, it seems that being shown how to check the whole word to see if it makes sense and looks right would help Kulsum improve her accuracy.
Monitoring and Correcting ■ Reread to problem-solve, self-correct, or confirm ■ Realize when more information is needed to understand a text	Kulsum rarely rereads to help problem-solve or self-correct. If she does reread, she only rereads a word and not a phrase. Kulsum would benefit from learning how to reread back to the beginning of the sentence or phrase which might allow her to problem- solve and self-correct more efficiently. Kulsum does not consistently realize that she might need more information in order to understand the text. This is demonstrated on page 4 when she substitutes *prate* for *pretty* and *sin* for *shiny.* She does not seem to make an attempt to find more information to

Figure 1.15   Behaviors and Understanding to Teach and Support: *Kulsum*

continues

KULSUM	
Behaviors and Understandings to Teach and Support (Guided Reading Continuum, Level G)	**Instructional Implications**
Monitoring and Correct, *cont.*	make her reading make sense. Her two attempts at the word *pretty* indicate that she knows she is not right but she does not look for more visual information to solve this word. She would benefit from instruction in how to reread and search for more information to solve words and confirm her reading.
Maintaining Fluency ■ Demonstrate phrased, fluent oral reading ■ Reflect language syntax and meaning through phrasing and expression ■ Reflect punctuation through appropriate pausing and intonation while reading orally	We see from Kulsum's fluency score of one that she reads primarily in two-word phrases with some three- and four-word groups and some word-by-word reading. She also reads with almost no expression or stress. She would benefit from demonstrations of how to read in larger, meaningful phrases as well as how to read punctuation with appropriate pausing and intonation.
Inferring ■ Infer causes and effects as implied in the text	From the comprehension conversation, it is evident that Kulsum is able to remember important facts and summarize what the text is about. However, it seems less clear that she is able to infer cause and effect. When prompted to talk about how bubbles get bigger, she explains that the more air they have the bigger they get. Though the text states, "Little bubbles have a little air inside. Big ones have more air inside," it does not explicitly state that bubbles become bigger when you put more air inside. Kulsum's statement that air, water and soap make them get bigger indicates that she has an idea of what happens, but wasn't able to fully infer the cause and effect.

Figure 1.15 Behaviors and Understanding to Teach and Support: *Kulsum (continued)*

©2011 by Irene Fountas & Gay Su Pinnell

Summary of Instructional Implications

Kulsum is demonstrating much effective problem-solving as a reader. She seems to understand her reading and is able to summarize many of the important details in a text. She would improve her accuracy significantly by learning how to notice and check the whole word and by being taught how to use what she knows about words and word parts to solve unknown words. These behaviors and understandings could easily be supported during text reading in guided reading, as well as during word work. Kulsum would also benefit from learning how to self-monitor when her reading does not make sense. By being taught to reread to problem-solve, monitor, and confirm her reading, Kulsum will be able to self-correct more consistently. She often uses multiple sources of information to solve words, so being taught to self-monitor when she needs more information and to reread to gain this information would enhance her ability to comprehend the text she is reading.

Give It a Try ▷

Individual Study

Plan time to listen to your own students read and discuss texts individually. Whether you are using Benchmark Assessment, running records, or another assessment tool, use the Guided Reading continuum to help you think about what behaviors and understandings they demonstrate and how they need to grow as readers.

Small Group Study & Staff Developers

If you are meeting with colleagues over time, have everyone focus on one student in each of their classes as a case study. Ask them to bring the reading assessments for that particular student, analyze them using the Guided Reading continuum, and share next steps with the group. Set up sessions where you focus as a group on these case studies and watch each readers' progress over time.

DVD 2

Interactive Read-Aloud and Literature Discussion

In this section of the Teaching Library, you will have the opportunity to explore how to use the Continuum to support your instruction during interactive read-aloud and literature discussion. For students in prekindergarten through grade one, most literature discussion actually takes place during interactive read-aloud during which the teacher reads an age-appropriate, grade-appropriate text aloud to the students and provides several opportunities to stop and discuss aspects of the text. As students become more proficient in talking about texts, they can begin to participate in small group discussions about texts (often called book clubs). For book clubs, students usually choose from texts the teacher has preselected and made accessible to all readers in a variety of ways, including reading them aloud or providing an audio recording of the text for those who can't access it on their own.

Although you do not need to consider the level of the text for the purposes of interactive read-aloud or literature study, text selection is still an important part of the process of planning interactive read-aloud and literature discussion. In both contexts, consider the text characteristics not only to determine if the text is age and grade appropriate, but also to decide whether the text has the potential to extend students' thinking and their ability to talk about texts. Are the texts rich with ideas to discuss? More importantly, consider how your teaching in these contexts will get students thinking within, beyond, and about texts in a variety of genres and formats.

For more detailed information about the Interactive Read-Aloud and Literature Discussion continuum, play the introduction to DVD 2 and read the introductory materials for Interactive Read-Aloud and Literature Discussion in *The Continuum of Literacy Learning, Grades PreK–8* or *PreK–2.* After playing the introduction, follow the suggested sequence of study below to learn how to use the Interactive Read-Aloud and Literature Discussion continuum as an assessment and planning tool.

Research ▷

Interactive read-aloud and literature discussion provide the foundation for text talk in the classroom. Besides building community and a common language around texts, interactive read-aloud and literature discussion provide a space for students to hear and discuss a variety of texts that they might not be able to access on their own. Through routines like "turn and talk" and the integration of text sets, students build their background knowledge and experience talking about texts in a variety of ways. To deepen your understanding of these instructional approaches, read more about them in Fountas and Pinnell's *Teaching for Comprehending and Fluency*. In addition to reading, try out some of the ideas you learn in these chapters in your own classroom. Trying these instructional approaches will help you better understand how to utilize the Interactive Read-Aloud and Literature Discussion continuum and will make watching the teaching segments on the DVD more meaningful.

Teaching for Comprehending and Fluency, Fountas and Pinnell, Heinemann, 2006

- Chapter 15: "Engaging Readers in Thinking and Talking about Texts Through Interactive Read-Aloud"

- Chapter 16: "Creating a Literate Culture Through Interactive Read-Aloud: Shared Talk About Texts"

- Chapter 17: "Planning for Interactive Read-Aloud and Literature Study Across the Grades"

- Chapter 18: "Moving From Interactive Read-Aloud to Literature Study"

- Chapter 19: "Deepening Comprehension: Engaging Students in Small-Group Literature Discussion"

- Chapter 20: "Getting Started With Book Clubs: Thinking and Talking About Texts"

Select a Clip and Print Supporting Materials ▷

Select examples from the clip descriptions below that are close to the grade levels in which you are interested. Text analyses of each book used in the teaching segments on the DVD are provided in the Preview section of the User Guide and can be printed from the PDF Resources link on the DVD.

DVD Clip Descriptions

Kindergarten Interactive Read-Aloud, *Ask Nicely:* In this segment, a teacher reads the fiction text *Ask Nicely* to her kindergarten class. The children bring background knowledge to the text, infer characters' feelings, interpret illustrations, and learn new vocabulary, as well as exhibit other important early behaviors.

First Grade Interactive Read-Aloud, *One Tiny Turtle:* A first grade class listens to their teacher read *One Tiny Turtle*, a nonfiction text. They learn about the structure of the text, notice new information, and actively engage in talking and listening.

First Grade Interactive Read-Aloud, *My Best Friend:* These first graders participate in an interactive read-aloud of the fiction text, *My Best Friend*. The children make predictions, infer the characters' feelings, and make connections to their own lives.

First Grade Interactive Read-Aloud, *Chester's Way:* The teacher reads the fiction text *Chester's Way* to her first-grade class. They make connections to other texts, make predictions, and compare and contrast characters.

Second Grade Interactive Read-Aloud, *Grandma's Purple Flowers:* Second graders listen to the emotional fiction text *Grandma's Purple Flowers,* talk about the writer's craft, interpret illustrations, and infer characters' feelings.

First Grade Literature Discussion, *Julius, The Baby of the World:* A group of first graders discuss the fiction text *Julius, the Baby of the World.* They connect the problems in the story to their own lives and offer evidence to support their thinking about characters' feelings and intentions.

Second Grade Literature Discussion, *Roller Coaster:* In this segment, a second grade group participates in their very first book club. As they discuss the book, *Roller Coaster,* they make personal connections to the topic, describe the plot, and examine the writer's craft and character change.

PDF Resources

MATERIALS FOR VIEWING TEACHING SEGMENTS

- Text Analysis of *Ask Nicely*
- Text Analysis of *One Tiny Turtle*
- Text Analysis of *My Best Friend*
- Text Analysis of *Chester's Way*
- Text Analysis of *Grandma's Purple Flowers*

MATERIALS FOR EXTENDING UNDERSTANDING

- Text Analysis Form

Preview ▷

Begin playing the clip for the lesson you have selected and pause when the authors suggest examining the *Selecting Texts* and *Selecting Goals* sections of the Interactive Read-Aloud and Literature Discussion continuum. See the suggestions below for more in-depth study of these sections.

Selecting Texts and Selecting Goals

Before watching the interactive read-aloud lessons you have selected, take a moment to look over the analysis of the characteristics of the text used in each lesson. For a more detailed description of each of these characteristics, see the introduction to Interactive Read-Aloud and Literature Discussion in *The Continuum of Literacy Learning, Grades PreK–8,* or *PreK–2.* The text analyses in Figures 2.1, 2.2, 2.3, and 2.4 were completed using the Interactive Read-Aloud and Literature Discussion continuum as a guide. In addition to helping determine the age and grade appropriateness of the text, the *Selecting Texts* section also helps you think about what aspects of the text may be supportive or challenging for your readers as you process the text together. Keeping in mind that you will be decoding the text during interactive read-aloud, you will need to think about what other behaviors and understandings might need support for your students to negotiate these characteristics and fully process the text.

Note: If you are focusing on literature discussion, you may want to take a moment to read through an analysis of the interactive read-aloud text below to familiarize yourself with the process of text analysis. Even though we have not included text analyses for the texts used in the literature discussion segments, you will want to consider the same factors in selecting texts for either instructional context.

 Individual Study

1. Print out the text analyses from the DVD or read through the analysis below for the interactive read-aloud lesson you have selected and think about how paying attention to the different characteristics of text will help you choose books to use in interactive read-aloud and literature discussion.

2. Now turn to S*electing Goals: Behaviors to Notice, Teach, and Support* for the grade level segment you are planning to watch. Scan the list of behaviors to become familiar with the bullets so that you can identify behaviors and understandings that you observe in the children's talk, those the teacher attends to in the lesson, and those that may be the focus of future instruction. *Thinking about some of the potential supports and challenges from the text analyses you have examined, what behaviors and understandings do you think the teacher might need to support as she reads and discusses this text with her students?* (Of course, you will need to use what you know about your own students in order to make these instructional decisions but thinking about these behaviors and understandings before watching the clip will help you identify them as you watch.)

 Small Group Study & Staff Developers

1. If you are a member of a small group or leading a professional development seminar, consider printing the text analysis for the teaching lesson you will be watching from the DVD to hand out to the group. Discuss with colleagues which characteristics listed in this analysis might be supportive or challenging for a typical student in this grade. *What will the teacher probably want to address and support as she reads this story?*

2. Keeping in mind the potential supports and challenges of the texts used in these clips, now turn to the S*electing Goals: Behaviors to Notice, Teach, and Support* for the grade level segment you are planning to watch. Scan the list of behaviors to become familiar with the bullets so that you can identify behaviors and understandings that you observe in the children's talk, those the teacher attends to in the lesson, and those that may be the focus of future instruction.

3. With a partner, discuss what behaviors and understandings you think the teacher might need to support as she reads and discusses this text with her students. (Of course, you will need to use what you know about your own students in order to make these instructional decisions but thinking about these behaviors and understandings before watching the clip will help you identify them as you watch.)

Text Analyses and Possible Teaching Points

This section includes a text analysis for each book used in the interactive read-aloud teaching segments on the DVD as well as a brief summary of the possible instructional implications of using this text.

Text Analysis: *Ask Nicely*

Text Factor	Analysis
Genre and Form	■ Realistic Fiction ■ Form: Picture Book
Text Structure	■ Simple structure with beginning, series of episodes, and an ending ■ Repetition of episodes and refrains ■ Repeating pattern
Content	■ Language and word play (the giant shook his fist, the giant stamped his foot, the giant yelled and howled) ■ A few topics beyond children's immediate experiences (giant, little boy helping big giant)
Themes and Ideas	■ Humor that is easy to grasp (silly giant) ■ Obvious themes (manners)
Language and Literary Features	■ Simple plots with clear problems and resolutions ■ Memorable characters ■ Characters change for reasons that are clear within the text (giant learned to be polite and to use his manners if he wants help) ■ Multiple characters ■ Rhythm and Repetition ("'Come here,' roared the giant," and "'No way!' said the _____.") ■ Simple dialogue easily attributed to characters ■ Memorable language or dialogue that is repeated ("Come here" and "No way")
Sentence Complexity	■ Sentences that children would use in oral conversation
Vocabulary	■ Some words of high interest that will be memorable to children (*roared, No way! Please*) ■ Many words that are in children's speaking vocabulary ■ A few new content words related to concepts that are easy to explain (*prickle, butcher, baker, grocer*) ■ Letters as words (*OK*)

Figure 2.1   Text Analysis: *Ask Nicely*

continues

Text Factor	Analysis
Text Analysis: *Ask Nicely*	
Words	▪ N/A
Illustrations	▪ Large, clear, colorful illustrations ▪ Illustrations that offer high support for comprehension
Book and Print Features	▪ Large print for children to see during read-aloud ▪ Title, author, and illustrator on cover but not on title page ▪ 16 pages in length ▪ Quotation marks, exclamation point, period ▪ Bold print ▪ All capital letters for emphasis

Figure 2.1   Text Analysis: *Ask Nicely (continued)*

Instructional Implications— Behaviors and Understandings to Notice, Teach, and Support

As you can see from the analysis of characteristics in Figure 2.1, *Ask Nicely* is perfectly suited for kindergarten-aged children. In this text, a silly giant forgets his manners as he confronts several characters throughout the story, demanding that they help him remove a splinter from his toe. The simple structure and repeating episodes and refrains invite children to predict what is coming next and help them easily identify the problem and solution in the story. The humor in the story is easy to grasp as is the overall theme about remembering to use one's manners. Though supported by illustrations, the vocabulary in the book may offer some kindergarten students a challenge, while also providing the opportunity to use context to determine the meaning of new content words.

Text Analysis: *One Tiny Turtle*

Text Factor	Analysis
Genre and Form	■ Hybrid text (a narrative with informational text embedded in it) ■ Form: Informational Picture Book
Text Structure	■ Informational text that includes both a simple narrative structure with beginning, series of episodes, and an ending, and facts in a separate font on the same page as the narration
Content	■ Familiar topic (turtles) ■ Content beyond most students' immediate experience (life cycle of a loggerhead turtle)
Themes and Ideas	■ Some themes going beyond everyday events (loggerhead turtle survival)
Language and Literary Features	■ Turtles that change for reasons that are clear within the text (life cycle of a loggerhead turtle) ■ Some literary language that is easy to understand ("Far, far out to sea, land is only a memory, and empty sky touches the water." "This is the nursery of a sea turtle.")
Sentence Complexity	■ Sentences that are more complex than children would use in one conversation ("Just beneath the surface is a tangle of weeds and driftwood where tiny creatures cling.") ■ A few sentences that are long with embedded phrases and clauses ("She pokes her pinprick nostrils through the silver surface to take a quick breath, so fast, blink and you'd miss it.")
Vocabulary	■ Some words of high interest that will be memorable to children (*pinprick, loggerhead, skitter*) ■ Many words that are in children's speaking vocabulary ■ A few new content words related to concepts children are learning and that are easy to explain (*loggerhead, lagoon, reptile, hatchlings, compass, horizon, armor*)
Words	■ N/A

Figure 2.2 Text Analysis: *One Tiny Turtle*

continues

Text Analysis: *One Tiny Turtle*	
Text Factor	**Analysis**
Illustrations	■ Large, clear, colorful illustrations in acrylic ■ Illustrations that offer high support for comprehension
Book and Print Features	■ Large print for children to see during read-aloud ■ The illustrations and the print engage the reader because there are two types of print: left to right large print for the narrative and narrower, wavy print (like the waves in the sea) that presents facts about the life cycle of loggerhead turtles ■ Title, author, and illustrator on cover and title page ■ Glossary

Figure 2.2   Text Analysis: *One Tiny Turtle (continued)*

Instructional Implications— Behaviors and Understandings to Notice, Teach, and Support

As described on the DVD, *One Tiny Turtle* is a fairly complex nonfiction text, with a challenging text structure that weaves together narrative and factual information. Though the text structure and large number of content words might be challenging for most first graders, the clear and colorful illustrations help support readers as they process this text. Additionally, the subject of the text— loggerhead turtles—is highly engaging for this age group, which will also facilitate their comprehension. Some of the complexities of the text will be mitigated by the fact that the teacher will be reading the text to the students; however, she will need to think about how to support her students in gathering information through both narrative and information reporting.

Text Analysis: *My Best Friend*

Text Factor	Analysis
Genre and Form	■ Realistic Fiction ■ Form: Picture Book
Text Structure	■ Simple narrative structure with beginning, series of episodes, and an ending
Content	■ Everyday events (playing with best friends, swimming, family)
Themes and Ideas	■ Obvious themes (friendship, acceptance, rejection)
Language and Literary Features	■ Simple plot with clear problems and resolutions (first grade main character wants a certain second grader to be her best friend) ■ Memorable characters in realistic story ■ Characters that change for reasons that are clear within the text ■ Multiple characters ■ Some figurative language that is easy to understand ("Whale Girl," "like bites out of a cookie") ■ Simple dialogue easily attributed to speakers
Sentence Complexity	■ Sentences that are more complex than children would use in oral conversation ■ A few sentences that are long with embedded phrases and clauses
Vocabulary	■ Some words of high interest that will be memorable to children (*scoops, behind*) ■ Many words that are in children's speaking vocabulary ■ A few new content words related to concepts children are learning and that are easy to explain (e.g., *cornrows*)
Words	■ N/A
Illustrations	■ Large, clear, colorful watercolor illustrations ■ Illustrations that offer high support for comprehension
Book and Print Features	■ Title, author, and illustrator on cover and title page

Figure 2.3   Text Analysis: *My Best Friend*

Instructional Implications— Behaviors and Understandings to Notice, Teach, and Support

My Best Friend, written by Mary Ann Rodman and illustrated by E.B. Lewis, is a simple narrative about everyday events that first graders can easily understand. In this story, first grader Lily wants to be best friends with second grader Tamika, who is more interested in playing with her second grade friend, Shanice, who is not very accepting of Lily. The themes of friendship and wanting to belong will provide most first graders with the opportunity to connect their own lives to the story. These personal connections can be used as an entryway for learning how to infer what the characters might be feeling and why they might be acting the way that they do. In most first-grade classrooms, this deep thinking beyond the text will need to be supported through talk throughout the read-aloud. Though some of the figurative language in the story may need support from the teacher, most can be grasped through the illustrations and context. The simple narrative structure and memorable characters will help first graders predict what is going to come next in the story and help them get inside the heads of the characters.

Text Analysis: *Chester's Way*

Text Factor	Analysis
Genre and Form	■ Fiction: Simple Animal Fantasy ■ Form: Picture Book
Text Structure	■ Simple narrative structure with beginning, series of episodes, and an ending ■ Story with repeating pattern
Content	■ Everyday events (eating, playing with friends, changing seasons, games, riding bikes) ■ Familiar topics (animals, families, food, school, friends, new person in the neighborhood)
Themes and Ideas	■ Humor that is easy to grasp ■ Obvious themes (friendship, new friend in the neighborhood, accepting differences)
Language and Literary Features	■ Simple plot with clear problems and resolutions ■ Memorable characters in animal fantasy ■ Characters who change for reasons that are clear within the text (learning about and accepting new friends with differences) ■ Multiple characters

Figure 2.4 Text Analysis: *Chester's Way*

continues

Text Analysis: *Chester's Way*

Text Factor	Analysis
Language and Literary Features, *cont.*	■ Some figurative language that is easy to understand ("two peas in a pod") ■ Simple dialogue easily attributed to speakers
Sentence Complexity	■ Sentences that are more complex than children would use in oral conversation ■ A few sentences that are long with embedded phrases and clauses
Vocabulary	■ Some words of high interest that will be memorable to children (*wheelie, double knots, talked backwards*) ■ Many words that are in children's speaking vocabulary ■ A few new content words related to concepts children are learning and that are easy to explain (*nifty disguise, hand signals, conversation, diagonally, personal remarks, miniature*)
Words	■ N/A
Illustrations	■ Large and small clear, colorful illustrations in watercolor and a black pen line ■ Illustrations that offer high support for comprehension
Book and Print Features	■ Some special features in the illustrations and print that engage interest and make texts interactive (speech—without bubble, illustration in a circle, and varying sizes of illustrations) ■ Title, author, and illustrator on cover and title page

Figure 2.4   Text Analysis: *Chester's Way (continued)*

Instructional Implications— Behaviors and Understandings to Notice, Teach, and Support

Chester's Way by Kevin Henkes has many characteristics that would be supportive for most first graders as they learn to discuss texts. The theme of making new friends and familiar topics such as school, playing, etc., make this text highly accessible to students of this age. The simple narrative structure with a beginning, series of episodes, and ending will support readers in understanding the problem in the story and its resolution. First graders may need support in thinking about character development and the change the two main characters undergo as they learn to accept a new friend into their neighborhood. In talking about the text, the teacher may also need to help them infer how the characters are feeling and why they act the way they do.

Text Analysis: *Grandma's Purple Flowers*

Text Factor	Analysis
Genre and Form	■ Memoir ■ Form: Picture Book
Text Structure	■ Simple structure with beginning, series of episodes, and an ending
Content	■ Content that verifies as well as extends students' experiences ■ Centers on issues related to family (love of a grandparent, death of a loved one) ■ Content that reflects African American and Southern cultures
Themes and Ideas	■ Themes important to second graders (friendship, family, neighborhood) ■ Most themes explicitly stated or easy to derive
Language and Literary Features	■ Story with multiple characters ■ Literary language, including some use of metaphor and simile, as well as description ("sun winks at me," "her smile grows wide like the Mississippi River," "The bright oranges and reds perform over my head," "The bare branches above stretch out like long fingers reaching for the sun.") ■ A few literary devices (story within a story: story of death and loss within a story about life and changing seasons) ■ Some complex vocabulary words that may or may not be understandable given students' background knowledge (*Mississippi River, hyacinth,* and *Sassafras*)
Sentence Complexity	■ Many long sentences with embedded clauses ("A leaf circles to the ground in back of Grandma's house where we used to plant collard greens and okra.") ■ Literary uses of language that increase sentence complexity ("When winter comes, cottony snowflakes dance around me as I walk through the park and down the hill to Grandma's house.")

Figure 2.5   Text Analysis: *Grandma's Purple Flowers*

continues

Text Analysis: *Grandma's Purple Flowers*	
Text Factor	**Analysis**
Vocabulary	■ Some words of high interest that will be memorable to children (*Mississippi, carnival colors, snowflakes, spooky*) ■ Many words that are in children's speaking vocabulary ■ New vocabulary words that are explained in the text or shown in illustrations (*hyacinth, sassafras tea, collard greens*)
Words	■ N/A
Illustrations	■ More complex illustrations that have detail and add more to the meaning of the text (cut paper collage with watercolors and acrylics) ■ Illustrations that reflect the theme and writer's tone and make a coherent work of art ■ Illustrations that help the reader understand the mood of the story
Book and Print Features	■ Title, author, and illustrator on cover and title page

Figure 2.5   Text Analysis: *Grandma's Purple Flowers (continued)*

Instructional Implications— Behaviors and Understandings to Notice, Teach, and Support

One of the characteristics of content in grade two books is that it can verify as well as extend students' experiences. *Grandma's Purple Flowers* (Figure 2.5) is such a book. While the theme of a grandparent's love and relationship with a child will be familiar and accessible to many students, the concept of losing a family member to death may or may not be within their experience. The metaphor of the changing seasons and the passage of time in the grandmother's life may be challenging for most second graders. This book also contains beautiful literary language which may

present a challenge as students try to comprehend the details of the story. While the illustrations in this story are supportive for understanding what is happening in the story, they also provide opportunities for students to gain more information than what is in the text. The teacher in this segment will have to keep these supports and challenges in mind while choosing what behaviors and understandings to support and teach through the reading of this story.

View Without Commentary ▷

View the lessons you have chosen **without commentary** keeping in mind the behaviors and understandings you previewed as well as the characteristics of the texts used in these clips. Take notes to help you remember what the teacher and students attend to as well as evidence of the students' learning.

- What behaviors and understandings is the teacher supporting or teaching for?
- What behaviors and understandings are the students demonstrating?

Think and/or Discuss

Pause the video segment before watching the lesson with commentary to think about and/or discuss what you observed.

 Individual Study

If you are working alone, review your notes and write down some of the behaviors or understandings you may have noticed as you watched the lesson.

 Small Group Study

If you are working with a group, discuss what behaviors and understandings you noticed in the lesson.

Revisit the Continuum

 Small Group Study & Staff Developers

After you have done your own thinking, reopen the Continuum to the section you viewed earlier.

- Identify the specific bulleted behaviors and understandings you noticed the students demonstrating.
- Identify the specific bulleted behaviors and understandings you noticed the teacher teaching for or supporting throughout the lesson.

View With Commentary

Now, play the teaching segment **with commentary** and compare what you have observed and discussed with the analysis on the DVD.

 Individual Study

Think about how your new understandings about the Interactive Read-Aloud and Literature Discussion continuum will impact your teaching.

- How will what you learned in this section impact your teaching of reading? What will you change tomorrow? What will you change over the course of the next few months?

 Small Group Study & Staff Developers

After viewing the clip with commentary, have the group talk about how they will use the Interactive Read-Aloud and Literature Discussion continuum in their teaching.

- What have you learned from the lesson(s) you watched and the conversations you have shared that will influence your teaching?

Extend

Selecting Texts and Planning Interactive Read-Aloud

 Individual Study

1. Choose a book you have read aloud to your students before.

2. Analyze the text with new eyes using the *Selecting Texts* section for your grade level. You may want to use the Text Analysis Form printable from the DVD under PDF Resources to support this analysis. *Does the book seem*

to match the characteristics described in this section? *What will be the demands of this text on your readers?*

3. Now, scan the bullets under the *Selecting Goals* section for the behaviors and understandings to notice, teach, and support. Think about the readers in your class. How would you need to support them to extend their thinking as readers?

4. Think about how you would change the way you read this book to your class. What behaviors and understandings would you want to support through this book? What would that look like in your teaching?

 Small Group Study

1. Have each group member bring a book they have read aloud to their class.

2. Choose two or three of the books (perhaps one for each grade level) to focus on. Read aloud the books to the group. (To save time, you may want to just pass the books around for people to review.)

3. Spend some time thinking about the demands of this text on readers. Compare the book to the characteristics of texts for the grade level for which you would use this text. *Do the characteristics seem to match the grade level characteristics in the continuum?*

4. Now scan the *Selecting Goals* section for that grade level. Ask group members who work with the grade you have selected to share the behaviors and understandings they feel they need to support their students in learning. As a group, pick three bulleted behaviors you may try to teach for or support through the text.

5. Discuss the following questions:

   ■ How will you support your students in expanding their thinking?

   ■ During the discussion of this book (in either interactive read-aloud or literature discussion), what will you be looking for as evidence of understanding?

 Staff Developers

1. If you are working with a large group, divide into smaller groups of three or four. Provide each group with a selection of books. Try to select books that represent a variety of genres and grade levels.

2. Have participants either share the selections with each other by taking turns reading them aloud or give them time to pass them around and read them to themselves.

3. Ask participants to put the books in order from easiest to most demanding and select a grade or grade range for each book.

4. Have each group choose one book for deeper analysis. Ask them to turn to the *Selecting Texts* section for the grade level they have selected and compare the book to the bulleted characteristics. You may want them to use the Text Analysis Form found in PDF Resources on DVD 2 to facilitate this analysis.

5. Once they have determined the supports and demands of the text, have them turn to the *Selecting Goals* section and think about three understandings they might decide to teach or support through this text.

6. Have each group share their findings with the larger group.

Connecting Continua

   Individual, Small Group & Staff Developers

Take a moment now to scan the list of bullets in the *Selecting Goals* section of the Oral, Visual, and Technological Communication continuum.

- What goals from this continuum have been met in the lessons you viewed of Interactive Read-Aloud and Literature Discussion?

Now turn to the Writing About Reading continuum in a grade level of your choice and scan the list of bullets for thinking within, beyond, and about text in the *Selecting Goals* section.

- In what ways have the lessons you viewed prepared students to respond to reading in writing?

- How have some of the goals of this section been met through the discussion in Interactive Read-Aloud and Literature Discussion? How are these continua interconnected?

- How can you see using Interactive Read-Aloud and Literature Discussion in preparation for Writing about Reading?

Lastly, take a moment to visit the Writing continuum at any grade level. Scan the goals specifically under *Craft*.

- How will the work done in Interactive Read-Aloud and Literature Discussion impact students as writers?

Give It a Try ▷

  Individual, Small Group & Staff Developers

Select a book you plan to read to your students for interactive read-aloud. Compare it to the *Selecting Texts* section of the Continuum to make sure it seems appropriate to your grade and to help you think about the demands and supports of the text. Look at the *Selecting Goals* section and select three or four understandings you plan to focus on during your interactive read-aloud. In choosing these goals, you will want to keep in mind the needs of the readers in your class as well as the supports and challenges offered by this book. Now, plan your interactive read-aloud: take four or five stick-on notes and place them throughout the book where you might make a comment, invite discussion, or ask a question.

 Individual Study

Take time to reflect on how this lesson went.

- What behaviors and understandings did your students seem to demonstrate during the read-aloud? How did you support these behaviors?

- What do you need to focus on next?

- How would you change your reading of this text the next time you read it aloud?

  Small Group Study & Staff Developers

If you are working in a group, you may want to break into grade level teams to do this planning. Have members of the group try the lesson in their own classrooms and then come back and talk about their experiences.

DVD 3

Shared and Performance Reading

In the introduction to the Shared and Performance Reading continuum on the DVD, you will learn how shared and performance reading is a valuable instructional context for all learners to expand their ability to read with comprehension and fluency. Whether students are participating in shared reading, choral reading, or readers' theater, students have the opportunity to:

- Process print in continuous text

- Work in a group (usually)

- Use their voices to interpret the meaning of text

- Read in unison with others or read an individual part

Most importantly, shared and performance reading involves thinking within, beyond, and about the text as readers interpret the text and try to communicate its meaning to their audience.

Take a moment to play the introduction to DVD 3 before continuing with the sequence of study that follows.

Research ▷

In addition to expanding the reader's ability to think within, beyond, and about text, shared and performance reading provides an authentic context for students to increase their fluency. To learn more about fluency and how to promote it through shared and performance reading, you may want to take time to explore the following chapters:

Teaching for Comprehending and Fluency, Fountas and Pinnell, Heinemann, 2006

- Chapter 6: "Understanding the Fluent Reader: Effective Processing"
- Chapter 7: " Recognizing Change Over Time in Fluent Reading"
- Chapter 21: "Promoting Shared and Performance Reading: Fluent Oral Processing of Texts"

Chapter 21 provides a detailed description of the elements of a shared reading lesson, procedures and tips for creating readers' theater scripts, as well as suggestions of texts across a variety of genres that are easily adapted for readers' theater.

Select a Clip and Print Supporting Materials ▷

Select a teaching segment from the DVD that is close to the text levels or grade level in which you are interested. **There are no supporting materials needed for this section of the User Guide.**

Video Segment Descriptions and Running Times

Prekindergarten Shared Reading, *Spots, Feathers, and Curly Tails:* A group of prekindergarten students reads the picture book *Spots, Feathers, and Curly Tails.* They search for and use information in the illustrations, learn new vocabulary, and begin to notice visual aspects of print. (15:05)

Kindergarten Shared Reading, "Here Are My Eyes": Kindergarten students read the poem "Here Are My Eyes." They work on voice-print match and quickly locate high-frequency words. (7:38)

First Grade Shared Reading, *The Enormous Watermelon:* First-grade students read from the big book *The Enormous Watermelon.* They interpret illustrations, make predictions, look for vowel patterns, and become more efficient word solvers by breaking down longer words. (25:05)

PDF Resources

There are no supporting materials needed for this DVD.

Preview ▷

Selecting Texts: Characteristics of Texts for Sharing and Performing

The Shared and Performance Reading continuum is organized in the same way as the Interactive Read-Aloud and Literature Discussion continuum with a section dedicated to text selection and goal selection. The *Selecting Texts* section provides guidelines for choosing appropriate texts for each grade level for shared and performance reading. Before watching the shared and performance reading clips, scan the list of characteristics for the grade you are focusing on. As mentioned in the introduction to the DVD, you will notice that in the earlier grades the texts are simple and often have an emphasis on rhythm and rhyme. At higher grade levels, you will see an emphasis on poetic or highly descriptive language. For more information on the ten text factors to consider in selecting books specifically for shared and performance reading, read the introductory materials about the Shared and Performance Reading continuum in *The Continuum for Literacy Learning, Grades PreK–8* or *PreK–2.*

Selecting Goals: Behaviors and Understandings to Notice, Teach, and Support

   Individual, Small Group & Staff Developers

Now, scan the bulleted behaviors and understandings to notice, teach, and support at the grade level for the teaching segment(s) you plan to watch. As with the other reading continua, the systems of strategic actions in this section are further divided into the categories of thinking within, beyond, and about the text. Think about how these behaviors and understandings apply to reading a text aloud either in shared reading, choral reading, or in readers' theater.

  Small Group Study & Staff Developers

If you are working in a group, discuss how shared and performance reading provides the opportunity to think within, beyond, and about the text. Select a few specific bulleted behaviors and understandings and discuss how shared and performance reading would help readers expand their thinking in this way. For example, how would readers' theater help one infer the feelings of a character? How might shared reading help readers recognize and identify aspects of text structure such as beginning and ending? How would readers' theater help students notice memorable language?

View Without Commentary ▷

Now, play the teaching segment you have chosen **without commentary**. As you record your observations, you may want to think about the following questions:

- What characteristics of the text used in this segment lend themselves to shared and performance reading?
- What behaviors and understandings do the students appear to be demonstrating?
- What behaviors and understandings do you notice the teacher supporting or teaching for?

Think and/or Discuss ▷

 Individual Study

If you are working alone, review your notes and try to specifically name some of the behaviors and understandings for which you saw evidence in the teaching and learning without looking in the Continuum.

  Small Group Study & Staff Developers

If you are working with a group, discuss what you noticed with your colleagues.

Revisit the Continuum ▷

After you have done your own thinking, reopen the Continuum to the section you viewed earlier.

- Identify the specific bulleted behaviors and understandings you noticed the students demonstrating.
- Identify the specific bulleted behaviors and understandings you noticed the teacher teaching for or supporting throughout the lesson.

View With Commentary ▷

Now, play the video segments **with commentary** and compare what you have observed and discussed with the analysis on the DVD. After you have completed this viewing, think about how you will use what you have learned in your own teaching.

 Individual Study

Think about how your new understandings about the Shared and Performance Reading continuum will impact your teaching.

- How will what you learned in this section impact your teaching of reading? What will you change tomorrow? What will you change over the course of the next few months?

 Small Group Study & Staff Developers

After viewing the clip with commentary, have the group talk about how they will use the Shared and Performance Reading continuum in their teaching.

- What have you learned from the lesson(s) you watched and the conversations you have shared that will help you in your teaching?

Extend ▷

You may choose to expand your study of the Shared and Performance Reading continuum by looking more closely at readers' theater and fluency.

 Individual & Small Group Study

Try to create your own readers' theater script using the *Selecting Texts* section of the Shared and Performance Reading continuum as a guide.

1. Choose a book you have read aloud to your students that you think might be conducive to performance reading and compare it to the text characteristics for the grade level with which you are working. You will want to think about books that have memorable language, rhythm or rhyme, or perhaps a repetitive refrain.

2. Select the parts to turn into dialogue and narrative and write the script. You may want to create this script with your students as a shared or interactive writing experience.

3. Select goals from the Shared and Performance Reading continuum *Selecting Goals* section that you will be looking for your students to demonstrate, as well as behaviors and understandings you will want to support or teach.

4. Assign parts and give your students the opportunity to have a fun and authentic experience reading text aloud.

 Staff Developers

Work in small groups to create a readers' theater script as described under the individual and small group study icon. Perform the scripts for one another. Ask other participants to use the Shared and Performance Reading continuum for the grade level for which you wrote this script to think about how your colleagues demonstrated thinking within, beyond, and about text while performing.

Connecting Continua

 Individual, Small Group & Staff Developers

Take a moment now to scan the list of bullets in the *Selecting Goals* section of the Oral, Visual, and Technological Communication continuum.

- What goals from this continuum have been met in the lessons you viewed of shared reading?

You will find more suggestions for extending your learning around fluency and shared and performance reading in the *Study Guide for The Continuum of Literacy Learning: A Guide to Teaching* at http://www.heinemann.com/shared/studyGuides/E01001/studyGuide.pdf. Ideas include resources for evaluating individual readers' fluency for which you can use the individual reader segments on DVD 1: Introduction and Assessment.

Give It a Try ▷

 Individual, Small Group & Staff Developers

1. Select a text using the Shared and Performance Reading continuum (e.g., big books, poems, readers' theater scripts) and evaluate it using the *Selecting Texts* section of the Shared and Performance Reading continuum.

2. Use the *Selecting Goals* section to choose two or three behaviors and/or understandings you plan to focus on through this reading

experience. Use what you know about your readers' strengths and needs from your reading assessments to make these choices and target your instruction.

3. While students are reading aloud as part of shared reading, choral reading, or readers' theater, keep open the *Selecting Goals* section of your Shared and Performance Reading continuum to help you think about what behaviors and understandings you see evidence for in their reading.

 Small Group Study & Staff Developers

After you have completed the shared and performance reading lesson, gather as a group to discuss what went well and what you would change for the future. Talk about how the Continuum helped in your planning and assessment for this particular lesson.

DVD 4

Writing About Reading

Throughout this DVD collection, you will notice the vast opportunities that students have to think and talk about texts. As they become increasingly comfortable responding to texts orally, they will be able to translate this response into written communication. Not only do writing and drawing about reading provide written evidence of your students' thinking, they also help them improve their ability to reflect on text and reciprocally develop their ability to talk about text.

It is important for your students to learn a variety of ways and purposes for communicating their thinking about texts. DVD 4 and this section of the User Guide help you explore the characteristics of the different forms of writing about reading and provide examples of how to familiarize your students with these characteristics. Shared and interactive writing provide a high level of support as teachers model how to construct responses to reading through functional, narrative, and informational writing. The introductory section of the DVD as well as the introductory matter in all of the versions of *The Continuum of Literacy Learning* give more details about these different forms of writing about reading as they apply to prekindergarten–grade 2.

The Teaching Library examples focus specifically on the use of interactive writing to introduce and teach students how to write about their reading. **Interactive writing** is an instructional approach in which the teacher and students compose a text together sharing the responsibility of scribe. During an interactive writing lesson, you invite a student to come up to the easel to contribute a letter, word, or part of a word in order to make a teaching point that helps students attend to various letters and words. These co-constructed writing pieces then become models or mentor texts that students can refer to as they begin to write about reading independently.

As in other instructional contexts, children acquire multiple understandings from each experience with writing about reading. They extend their comprehension of texts, developing the behaviors and understandings detailed in the Interactive Read-Aloud and Literature Discussion continuum, as well as the Guided Reading continuum. They learn about the craft, conventions, and the writing process (as detailed in the Writing continuum) and have the opportunity to learn about letters, sounds, and how words work (drawing on the Phonics, Spelling, and Word Study continuum). For our observations of the teaching segments in DVD 4, we draw from several of the continua and will suggest how you can integrate them into your planning as you help your students respond to their reading in writing.

Play the introduction to DVD 4: Writing About Reading for more details about the content and organization of the Writing About Reading continuum. Then, follow the suggested sequence of study to learn more about how to use this continuum in your planning and assessment of writing about reading.

Research ▷

For more information about the value of writing about reading and how to transition your students from talking about texts to writing about them in a variety of genres, read the chapters in the following texts:

Teaching for Comprehending and Fluency, Fountas and Pinnell, Heinemann, 2006

- Chapter 27: "Writing About Reading: Moving from Talk to Written Conversation About Texts"
- Chapter 28: "Writing About Reading in a Variety of Genres"

When Readers Struggle: Teaching That Works, Pinnell and Fountas, Heinemann, 2009

- Chapter 13: "Extending Reading Power Through Writing"

Guiding Readers and Writers, Fountas and Pinnell, Heinemann, 2001

- Chapter 10: "Writing to Explore Meaning: Reader's Notebook" (particularly helpful for grade 2 and up)

Interactive Writing, McCarrier, Pinnell, and Fountas, Heinemann, 2000

- Chapter 9: "Exploring and Extending the Meaning of Literature"

Note: *Interactive Writing* by McCarrier, Pinnell, and Fountas also provides detailed information about the components of an interactive writing lesson and how to use interactive writing in your classroom in a variety of contexts.

Select a Clip and Print Supporting Materials ▷

You may decide to watch all of the clips on this DVD or choose one or two examples that apply to the grade level for which you are interested. Scan the list of supporting materials under PDF Resources below. Print any materials you plan to use by putting the DVD in your computer and clicking on PDF Resources.

Video Segment Descriptions and Running Times

Kindergarten Interactive Writing About Reading, *The Snowy Day:* Kindergarten students write about what a character in *The Snowy Day* sees throughout the book. The children notice visual patterns in words and make connections between words. (13:40)

Kindergarten Interactive Writing About Reading, *Tops and Bottoms:* Kindergarten students think about a story their class read previously during interactive read-aloud and write advice to one of the characters in the book, *Tops and Bottoms.* Students practice the format of a letter and try several word-solving strategies. (20:39)

First Grade Interactive Writing About Reading, *Sheila Rae, The Brave:* A first grade class writes a response to *Sheila Rae, The Brave*. As they write a letter to the main character of the story, they have the opportunity to think about the events of the story and what the character should have done differently. (14:01)

First Grade Interactive Writing about Reading, *The Moon:* First graders in this class write a sentence that explains two things they learned about the moon from their reading. In the segment, they work with words that have two vowels in the middle of them and break down two-syllable words. (23:41)

PDF Resources

MATERIALS FOR VIEWING TEACHING SEGMENTS

- Observing Writing About Reading form

MATERIALS FOR EXTENDING UNDERSTANDING (SEE EXTEND SECTION FOR DETAILS)

- Analyzing Writing About Reading form
- Writing About Reading Samples

KINDERGARTEN

- "The Hat" by Devon—Functional
- "The Hat" by Noah—Functional

FIRST GRADE

- "Dear Eric Carle"—Functional
- "Animals That Come From Eggs"—Informational

SECOND GRADE

- *Nate the Great* Letter—Functional
- *The Librarian From the Black Lagoon* Letter—Functional
- "Review of Rosa Parks"—Informational

Preview ▷

Before watching the teaching segments you have selected, take a moment to preview the Writing About Reading continuum for the grade level you will be watching.

Selecting Genres and Forms

Begin by turning to the *Selecting Genres and Forms* section of the Writing About Reading continuum for the selected grade level. Read over the different forms of writing about reading, which are organized into three categories for prekindergarten through grade 2: functional writing, narrative writing, and informational writing. Besides scanning the bullets under each category, it is helpful to read the introductory paragraph on this page. The introduction provides some guidelines and expectations for what writing about reading might look like for that grade level. Helping students identify the different characteristics of each of these forms of writing about reading during shared experiences and demonstrations (e.g,. interactive, shared, and modeled writing) will allow them to eventually use them independently to respond to their own books.

Selecting Goals: Behaviors and Understandings to Notice, Teach, and Support

Now, turn to the *Selecting Goals* page for the selected grade level. Scan the bullets under thinking within, beyond, and about the text to get an idea of the behaviors and understandings the readers in the classrooms on the DVD might demonstrate in response to books they have heard read aloud. Becoming familiar with these behaviors and understandings will also help you identify how the teaching moves in these segments support or teach the students to think in different ways.

Connecting Continua

Before watching the writing about reading clip you have selected, you also may want to take a few minutes to familiarize yourself with the organization and content of the Phonics, Spelling, and Word Study continuum. The behaviors and understandings in this continuum are integrated throughout the writing about reading teaching segments. The introduction on DVD 7, as well as the introductory materials of the Phonics, Spelling, and Word Study continuum in *The Continuum of Literacy Learning, Grades PreK–8* and *PreK–2*, provides an overview of the content and organization of the Phonics, Spelling, and Word Study continuum. Turn to the *Selecting Goals* page for the selected grade level and scan the list of bullets under each category before viewing the teaching segment you have chosen.

View Without Commentary ▷

After becoming familiar with the different sections of the Writing About Reading continuum, view the lesson(s) you have chosen **without commentary** using the suggestions below to focus your observations. If you choose, use the *Observing Writing About Reading* document found in PDF Resources to record your observations.

 Individual Study

Record your observations using the following questions to guide your thinking. You may want to view the video twice—once with a focus on the Writing About Reading continuum and the second time with a focus on the Phonics, Spelling, and Word Study continuum.

- What do the students seem to understand or to be learning about the genre or form of writing about reading featured in this teaching segment?

- What behaviors and understandings do you see evidence for in the students' responses?

- What behaviors and understandings do you see the teacher supporting through this lesson?

- What do the students seem to understand about the way words work? How is the teacher teaching for or supporting the students' understanding of phonics, spelling, and word study?

 Small Group Study & Staff Developers

Divide participants into two groups. Ask one group to focus on the types of behaviors and understandings related to the Writing About Reading continuum and the other group to think about the Phonics, Spelling, and Word Study continuum. Each group can focus their observations using the following questions as a guide:

- What behaviors and understandings did you notice the students demonstrating?

- What behaviors and understandings were taught or supported by the teacher?

Think and/or Discuss ▷

Pause the video segment before watching it with commentary to think about and/or discuss what you observed.

 Individual Study

If you are working alone, review your notes and write down some of the specific behaviors or understandings you may have noticed as you watched the lesson. Do your best to name what you have observed.

 Small Group Study & Staff Developers

If you are working with a group, discuss with colleagues what behaviors and understandings you noticed in the lesson.

Revisit the Continuum ▷

After you have done your own thinking, reopen the continuum to the sections you viewed earlier.

- Identify the specific bulleted behaviors and understandings you noticed the students demonstrating.

- Identify the specific bulleted behaviors and understandings you noticed the teacher teaching for or supporting throughout the lesson.

View With Commentary

Now, play the video segment **with commentary** and compare what you have observed and discussed with the analysis on the DVD. After you have completed this viewing, think about how you will use what you have learned in your own teaching.

 Individual Study

Think about how your new understandings about the Writing About Reading continuum will impact your teaching.

- How will what you learned in this section impact your teaching of reading and writing? What will you change tomorrow? What will you change over the course of the next few months?

 Small Group Study & Staff Developers

After viewing the teaching segment with commentary, have the group talk about how they will use the Writing About Reading continuum in their teaching.

- What have you learned from the lesson(s) you watched and the conversations you have shared that will help you in teaching your students to respond to their reading in writing?

Extend ▷

After experiencing writing (and drawing) about reading in different genres and forms several times with group support, students will be able to produce them on their own. As they begin writing about their reading independently, observe their writing and drawing for evidence of their thinking about text as well as their ability to write for a variety of purposes in different genres. There are writing about reading samples from a variety of grades and genres in the PDF Resources section of this DVD. To extend your understanding of how to use the Writing About Reading continuum as an assessment tool, print these samples and complete your own analysis using the steps below as a guide. You may want to use the document titled *Analyzing Writing About Reading* (also printable from PDF Resources) to facilitate your note taking. You will find complete analyses of a few of these pieces below, which can be used as examples to inform your analysis or as a means of comparison once you are done.

 Individual Study

1. Choose a sample from your grade level of interest and turn to the *Selecting Genres and Forms* section in the Writing About Reading continuum for that grade level. Begin by determining what type of writing about reading you are assessing.

2. Scan the *Selecting Goals* section and record the bullets that seem to apply to the piece of writing. Think about possible next steps for this student.

 Small Group Study & Staff Developers

1. Print out all of the samples of writing about reading and provide small groups with one of each sample. Have them divide the samples up and work in partners following the steps described for individual study.

2. Have partners share their findings within their group. Discuss the change over time in writing about reading. How do the behaviors and understandings from prekindergarten to grade 2 change and build upon one another?

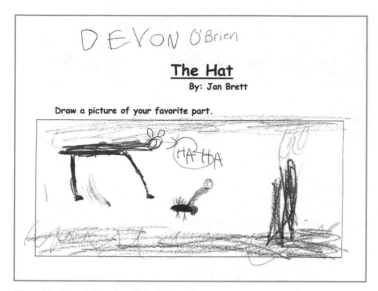

Figure 4.1   Devon's Drawing of *The Hat*

Figure 4.2   Writing About *Animals That Come From Eggs*

Dear Mrs. Skinvan,
    I reaed Nate the Great and the Missing Key. My favorite part was when Nate founed the key. The key was on Annies dog Fang. It was on his collar. My favorite character was Nate because he likes to sollve mysterys.
                    your student,
                    Cameron

Figure 4.3   Writing About *Nate the Great*

Student Work	Genre and Form	Behavioral Evidence (from the Writing About Reading Continuum)
"The Hat" by Devon (Figure 4.1) 	Functional Writing ▪ Sketches or drawings that reflect content of a text	**Kindergarten** *Thinking within the text* ▪ Represent a character through drawing and writing. (You can see the porcupine represented with the hat on his head.) ▪ Tell important information from a story. (Devon has chosen to highlight one of the most important parts of the story when the animals laugh at the Hedgehog.) ▪ Use text as a resource for words, phrases, and ideas. (e.g. *haha*) *Thinking beyond the text* ▪ Express opinions about stories or poems. (Devon is highlighting his favorite part.)
"Animals That Come From Eggs" (Figure 4.2) 	Informational Writing ▪ Short sentences and/or drawings of a sequence of actions or directions	**First Grade** *Thinking within the text* ▪ Write short sentences to report or summarize important details from a text. ▪ Notice and sometimes use new words from a text. (e.g. *tadpole*) ▪ Tell important information from a story. ▪ Reread to assure accuracy of sentence structure and word use as well as meaningfulness (e.g. she crosses out the *s* in *eggs* so the sentence makes sense). ▪ Use text as a resource for words, phrases and ideas. *Thinking beyond the text* ▪ Reflect both prior knowledge and new knowledge from the text.

Figure 4.4 Writing About Reading

continues

Student Work	Genre and Form	Behavioral Evidence (from the Writing About Reading Continuum)
"Animals That Come From Eggs," *cont.*		**Thinking about the text** ■ Create texts that have some of the characteristics of published texts (illustrations, diagram at the end). ■ Sometimes borrow the style or some language from a writer (e.g. questions—"Did you know a turtle comes from an egg?") ■ Notice the way a text is organized and sometimes apply organization for writing (e.g. illustration with a fact; lists a different animal that lays eggs on each page). ■ Produce some simple graphic representations of a story (e.g., diagram of the tadpole becoming a frog at the end of the story).
Nate the Great Letter by Cameron (Figure 4.3)	Functional Letter ■ Letters to other readers or to authors and illustrators (including dialogue letters in a reader's notebook)	**Second Grade** *Thinking within the text* ■ Accurately reflect information from a text. ■ Represent information, concepts, setting, events, characters, and story problems through drawing and/or writing. ■ Report information from a text or summarize it in a few sentences (e.g. summarize problem and solution—missing key found on Fang's collar). ■ Represent important information about a fiction text (characters, events) or informational text. (e.g. Nate the Great solves mysteries). *Thinking beyond the text* ■ Write opinions about a text and back them up with specific information or opinions (Cameron is starting to do this by expressing his favorite part of the story and providing some detail. His teacher might decide to build upon this ability by teaching him to communicate his reasons for picking a certain part as his favorite.)

Figure 4.4 Writing About Reading *(continued)*

Give It a Try ▷

 Individual, Small Group & Staff Developers

1. Choose one form of writing about reading from the *Selecting Genres and Forms* section of the Writing About Reading continuum to demonstrate to your students. Think about how you want to familiarize them with this genre of writing about reading (e.g. through interactive writing, shared writing, or modeled writing).

2. Select a text from interactive read-aloud to respond to in this particular genre.

3. Using the *Selecting Goals* section of the Writing About Reading continuum for the appropriate grade, scan the list of bullets and think about what behaviors and understandings you may want to support and teach for through this lesson. Remember, carefully consider what your students already know and how they need to grow as readers and writers when you select these goals.

4. Provide several examples in a group setting before asking students to try writing about their reading in the genre independently.

Writing: Focus on Interactive Writing

Whether you teach prekindergarten or second grade, the Writing continuum is a tool that can be used to help you create a classroom environment where writers can grow. The Writing continuum's complexity reflects the multiple ways you need to look at your students' writing and process as they attempt to communicate for different purposes through a variety of genres. The Introduction on DVD 5 and the Preview section below provide more detail about the organization and content of the Writing continuum.

Before students are expected to write in a new genre independently, they need multiple experiences with a genre. The exposure to different genres begins in shared experiences with text, particularly through interactive read-aloud. Consider organizing your interactive read-aloud texts into text sets around genre so your students are exposed to different texts within a genre over several days or weeks before they are expected to write in the genre. To learn more about how to develop these text sets, see Chapter 17 of Fountas and Pinnell's *Teaching for Comprehending and Fluency.* These shared texts will become mentor texts for your students as they embark on their own writing.

In addition to exposing students to different genres in reading, you need to demonstrate how to write in a variety of genres through **interactive writing, shared writing,** and **modeled writing**. DVD 5 focuses on the use of **interactive writing** to introduce and expose students to a variety of genres as well as to teach them about different aspects of craft, conventions, and the writing process. Interactive writing involves the teacher and student composing a piece of writing together, sharing the role of scribe. By inviting students to come up to the easel and contribute a letter, word, or part of a word, you also provide opportunities for children to learn a lot about the way words work. Since interactive writing provides natural opportunities for word study, you are encouraged to use the **Phonics, Spelling, and Word Study continuum,** as well as the Writing continuum, in viewing these segments and in your own planning of interactive writing. Another useful tool to have handy during this portion of the DVD is the *Fountas and Pinnell Prompting Guide, Part One* if you have it in your collection of professional resources.

For more information about shared or modeled writing, see the introductory materials of the Writing continuum in *The Continuum of Literacy Learning, Grades PreK–8* or *PreK–2.*

Research ▷

You may want to spend time reading about interactive writing and trying a few interactive writing lessons yourself to familiarize yourself with the procedures and elements of an interactive writing lesson. Understanding the structure and possible uses of interactive writing will help you focus your study of how to use the Writing continuum as a tool in planning your interactive writing lessons.

FOR MORE INFORMATION ON INTERACTIVE WRITING:

Interactive Writing, McCarrier, Pinnell, and Fountas, Heinemann, 1999

FOR MORE INFORMATION ON USING WRITING MENTORS AND CRAFTING WRITING:

Guiding Readers and Writers, Fountas and Pinnell, Heinemann, 2001

■ Chapter 25: "Exploring the Writer's Terrain: Writer Talks, Writer's Notebooks, and Investigations"

Select a Clip and Print Supporting Materials ▷

Select a lesson or lessons to view from the clip descriptions below that are close to the grade levels of interest to you.

Video Segment Descriptions and Running Times

Prekindergarten Interactive Writing Lesson, Captions for Self-Portraits: A group of prekindergarteners work on a simple form of interactive writing—the writing of their names. They are working on connecting beginning sounds to letters. (16:22)

Kindergarten Interactive Writing Lesson, Writing About a Brooder: These kindergarten children determine and write a sentence about putting chicks in a brooder. They connect new words to known words, learn that two letters can represent one sound, and engage in early reading behaviors. (20:58)

Kindergarten Interactive Writing Lesson, Writing a How-To Text: The children in this kindergarten class write a how-to text together about making a bird feeder with a bagel. They recall the steps required to make the feeder and work to put the information in a sequence. (15:44)

Grade 1 Interactive Writing Lesson, Writing About Plants: In this segment, the teacher works with a small group of first graders to write about what they have learned about plants. The segment demonstrates how to use the Writing continuum to plan instruction for small groups to teach students about craft, conventions, and the writing process. (14:42)

PDF Resources

There are no PDF resources for this section; however, you will find several writing samples from children in grades prekindergarten through grade 2 along with analyses of these pieces on DVD 6. See the Extend section of DVD 6 for more details on how to use these writing samples to expand your understanding of the Writing continuum.

Preview ▷

Begin by playing the introduction to **DVD 5: Writing: Focus on Interactive Writing** to gain an overview of the organization and content of the Writing continuum. The introductory matter to the Writing continuum in *The Continuum of Literacy Learning, Grades PreK–8* and *PreK–2* also provides a detailed description of the contents of this section.

To briefly review, the Writing continuum is divided into two overarching categories: *Selecting Purpose and Genre* and *Selecting Goals*. Since writing is multifaceted, these learning goals are further divided into three areas: **Craft, Conventions,** and **Writing Process**. After playing the introduction, pause the video segment, turn to the grade level for the clip you have selected, and take some time to become familiar with the bullets in each of these sections.

Selecting Purpose and Genre

Writers determine a purpose for their writing and then choose the genre that will best allow them to communicate their purpose. To facilitate your planning of instruction, the writing genres are categorized under four purposes (though we acknowledge virtually any genre can be used to support a given purpose). These four categories include: **narrative, informational, poetic,** and **functional**. Under each genre within these categories, there are two sets of information: *Understanding the Genre*, which reflects the key understandings that students need to know about the genre, and *Writing in the Genre*, which refers to the way the students demonstrate their understanding of this genre (what students *do* with the genre.)

- Scan the bullets in this section before viewing the teaching segment.

Selecting Goals: Behaviors and Understandings to Notice, Teach, and Support

As teachers of writing, we need to help the writers in our classrooms grow in their understanding of craft, conventions, and the writing process itself.

Craft: To craft an effective piece of writing, an author must organize and structure focused, well-developed ideas, use language appropriate for the genre, consider word choice, and reveal their own unique style through the voice of the piece. Accordingly, the goals in this section fall under the following categories: *Organization, Idea Development, Language Use, Word Choice,* and *Voice.*

- Scan the bullets under "Craft" for the grade level you have selected.

Conventions: The goals in this section focus on the following conventions of writing: *Text Layout, Grammar, Capitalization, Punctuation, Spelling,* and *Handwriting/Word Processing*. It is important to note that students will develop the conventions of writing over time. Conventions help writers to communicate their ideas clearly and are important particularly in the editing process.

- Scan the bullets under "Conventions" for the grade level you have selected.

Writing Process: As students produce pieces in a variety of genres and bring them through the writing process, they will grow in their understanding of this recursive process. The continuum contains goals within the four key phases of the writing process: *Rehearsing and Planning, Drafting and Revising, Editing and Proofreading,* and *Sketching and Drawing. Viewing Self as Writer* is also included in this section as it applies to all phases of the writing process.

- Scan the bullets under "Writing Process" for the grade level you have selected.

Connecting Continua

Before watching the interactive writing clip you have selected, take a few minutes to familiarize yourself with the organization and content of the Phonics, Spelling, and Word Study continuum. You will observe the integration of this continuum throughout the interactive writing segments. See the Phonics, Word Study and Spelling Preview section of DVD 7: The Phonics, Spelling, and Word Study continuum for more details. The introduction on DVD 7 as well as the introductory matter in *The Continuum of Literacy Learning, Grades Pre K–8* and *PreK–2* also provide an overview of the content and organization of the Phonics, Spelling, and Word Study continuum.

You may also want to preview the Oral, Visual, and Technological Communication continuum before viewing the clips you have selected as many of the behaviors and key understandings from this continuum are also observed, supported, and taught in these lessons.

View Without Commentary ▷

After becoming familiar with the different sections of the Writing continuum, view the lesson(s) you have chosen **without commentary** using the suggestions below to focus your observations.

 Individual Study

Record your observations using the following questions to guide your thinking. (Consider viewing the teaching segment twice—once with a focus on the students' writing behaviors and the second time with a focus on their understanding of phonics, spelling, and word study.)

- What behaviors are the students demonstrating throughout this lesson? What do they understand about writing?

- What writing behaviors and understandings do you see the teacher supporting or teaching for throughout this lesson?

- What do the students seem to understand about the way words work?

- How does the teacher support or teach for these behaviors and understandings?

 Small Group Study & Staff Developers

Divide participants into two groups.

- Ask one group to record the behaviors of the students and the teaching moves of the teacher that relate to the Writing continuum.

- What do the students seem to understand about writing?

- What is the teacher trying to teach them about writing through this interactive writing lesson?

- Have the other group focus on what the students' behaviors tell us about their understanding of concepts related to phonics, spelling, and word study. How is the teacher supporting or explicitly teaching for these behaviors and understandings?

Think and/or Discuss ▷

Pause the video segment before watching the section with commentary to think about and/or discuss what you observed.

 Individual Study

If you are working alone, review your notes and write down some of the specific behaviors or understandings you may have noticed as you watched the lesson. Do your best to name what you have observed.

 Small Group Study & Staff Developers

If you are working with a group, discuss what behaviors and understandings you noticed in the lesson with colleagues.

Revisit the Continuum ▷

After you have done your own thinking, reopen the continuum to the section you viewed earlier. (Use the continuum related to the grade level featured in the clip you watched.) You may want to focus on one particular aspect of the Writing continuum at a time or scan each section using the guidelines below.

- Scan the list of bullets under Selecting a Purpose or Genre.

  - What were the purpose and genre featured in the teaching clip you watched?

  - Identify any key understandings under Understanding the Genre and Writing in the Genre that you saw students demonstrate.

  - Identify the specific bulleted behaviors and understandings you noticed the teacher teaching for or supporting about genre through the interactive writing experience.

- Now turn to Selecting Goals: Behaviors and Understandings to Notice, Teach, and Support and scan the list of bullets under Craft and Conventions.

  - Identify the specific bulleted behaviors and understandings you noticed the students demonstrating.

  - Identify the specific bulleted behaviors and understandings you noticed the teacher teaching for or supporting throughout the lesson.

- Now turn to Selecting Goals: Behaviors and Understandings to Notice, Teach, and Support and scan the list of bullets under Writing Process.

  - What did the students in the clip you watched learn about the writing process?

Connecting Across Continua

You may also want to visit the Phonics, Spelling, and Word Study continuum as well as the Oral, Visual, and Technological Communication continuum to gain further insight into your observations. Scan the bulleted list of behaviors and understandings. Notice how you can integrate the goals of multiple continua in one lesson.

View With Commentary ▷

Now, play the video segment **with commentary** and compare what you have observed and discussed with the analysis offered on the DVD. After you have completed this viewing, think about how you will use what you have learned in your own teaching.

 Individual Study

Think about how your new understandings about the Writing continuum and interactive writing will impact your teaching.

- How will what you learned in this section impact your teaching of writing? What will you change tomorrow? What will you change over the course of the next few months?

 Small Group Study & Staff Developers

After viewing the clip with commentary, have the group talk about how they will use the Writing continuum in their teaching.

- What have you learned from the lesson(s) you watched and the conversations you have shared that will help you in your teaching?

Extend ▷

The Fountas and Pinnell Prompting Guide, Part 1: A Tool for Literacy Teachers will help you extend your understanding of how to translate the bulleted information in *The Continuum of Literacy Learning, Grades PreK–8* and *K–2* into specific language for noticing, teaching, and supporting students throughout reading and writing workshop. If you have this resource, this section will provide insight into how to use it as a tool in your instruction by helping you focus on the teacher's use of language throughout each teaching clip. Turn to the sections related to writing in *Prompting Guide, Part 1*.

  Small Group & Large Group

If you are working with a group of colleagues, assign partners or groups the different sections of the *Prompting Guide* related to early writing: composing sentences, early writing behaviors, verbal path for letter formation, constructing words, conventions, revisiting the text for word study. Watch the teaching segments you have selected and have groups record the specific language they noticed the teacher using.

Ask them to think about the following questions while watching and then discuss them after the viewing:

■ What different levels of support is the teacher offering?

■ When does she choose to teach, prompt, or reinforce a behavior or understanding?

■ How could you use this tool in your own teaching?

 Individual Study & Staff Developers

If you are working alone, choose to focus on one or two parts of the *Prompting Guide* at a time while watching the videos so you can really pay attention to the language the teachers use in the clips.

Note: The *Prompting Guide* can be integrated into your viewing of any of the teaching segments for reading and writing in this Teaching Library using the same process of observing teacher language described above. It is recommended that you first watch the videos for the behaviors and understandings as noted in the *The Continuum of Literacy Learning, Grades PreK–8* and *PreK–2* and then, to use the *Prompting Guide* to re-watch the clips as you focus on the teacher's use of specific language that supports the child's problem-solving.

Give It a Try ▷

1. Try using the Writing continuum in your planning of interactive writing.

2. Begin by choosing the new genre you plan to explore with your students using the *Selecting Purpose and Genre* section of the Writing continuum for the grade level you teach.

Note: Many times during interactive writing your students and you will choose the genre you plan to write in together as you discuss what you are going to write and think about the purpose for the writing. However, in the case that you are demonstrating how to write in a new genre, select and view the bullets in this section before your lesson.

3. Look over the list of what students will need to understand about this genre and what they will need to be able to do to write in the genre. How will you familiarize them with

these key understandings? How can you use your interactive read-alouds to begin the process of introducing this genre?

4. Scan the list of goals for Craft and Conventions and think about next steps for your students. What are they working on as writers? Where do you need to bring them next? Select one or two bullets from each area to keep in mind as you construct the text with your students.

5. Conduct the interactive writing lesson with your students.

6. Revisit the continuum at the end of your lesson and think about what behaviors and understandings your students demonstrated during this lesson and where you might bring them next as writers.

DVD 6

Writing: Focus on Writing Workshop

DVD 6 focuses on how to use the Writing continuum to facilitate your planning and assessment during writing workshop. Writing workshop is usually an hour-long block and follows the same structure each day:

1. **Minilesson** on any aspect of writing: Craft, Conventions, or Process (approximately 5–10 minutes)

2. **Individual Writing Time** during which you have individual conferences with students (approximately 30–40 minutes)

3. **Sharing** a brief time at the end of the workshop during which children talk about their work and the minilesson is usually revisited (approximately 5–10 minutes)

The teaching segments on this DVD allow you to visit writing workshops from beginning to end in three different first-grade classrooms and one second-grade classroom. Through each segment, you will see how the teacher is able to use the continuum as a planning and assessment tool in each instructional context—whether it is to plan the minilesson principle, assess a piece of student writing and select a teaching point during a conference, or guide the sharing time.

Research ▷

Through the video clips in this section, you will gain insight into the procedures and structures of a writing workshop. However, this DVD is designed to help you learn how to use the Writing continuum to enhance your established writing workshop. If you are just beginning writing workshop or need to refresh your understanding, please see the following resources for more information. The introductory matter in the Writing continuum, as well as the introduction on DVD 5, also provide details about writing in different genres and the writing process.

Guided Reading: Good First Teaching for All Children, Fountas and Pinnell, Heinemann, 1996

- Chapter 3: "Guided Reading Within a Balanced Literacy Program"

Guiding Readers and Writers, Fountas and Pinnell, Heinemann, 2001

- Chapter 5: "Developing Accomplished Writers: The Writing Workshop"
- Chapter 25: "Exploring the Writer's Terrain: Writer Talks, Writer's Notebooks, and Investigations"

Select a Clip and Print Supporting Materials ▷

Select an example from the DVD that is close to the grade level in which you are interested. There are multiple ways to use this section of the Teaching Library. It is recommended that you select at least one entire writing workshop to view from one classroom to get a complete perspective of how the Writing continuum can be used in multiple instructional contexts within writing workshop.

However, you might choose to revisit these teaching segments and focus on one aspect of the writing workshop at a time. For example, you may decide you want to explore writing minilessons in depth in which case you would choose a selection of minilessons from each workshop to view. Regardless of how you choose to view the teaching segments, you will be closely observing the behaviors and understandings that the students demonstrate and those that the teacher chooses to teach and support in each instructional setting.

Video Segment Descriptions and Running Times

Prekindergarten, Writing Workshop on Bookmaking: During a group minilesson (12:09), four-year-olds learn how to make a book about animals based on a mentor text. The book includes pictures of animals and descriptions of the sounds they make. The children learn about letter-sound relationships. In conferences (6:46), the children work on sequencing events and recognizing where information is missing.

Grade 1, Writing Workshop on Using Headings:

Minilesson: The teacher introduces how to use headings to organize informational writing to her first graders. She shows them mentor texts and helps them see how headings can guide readers. (17:34)

Conference with Alison: The teacher works with Alison on her informational text about Martin Luther King. They look at a timeline as a tool for finding information and add headings to the text. (7:47)

Conference with Sana: The teacher works with Sana on how to write headings to organize her writing and then helps her think about how she will revise the piece. (6:43)

Share: The teacher shares several examples from the children's work to reinforce their understanding of the use of headings. (7:21)

Grade 1, Writing Workshop on Writing "How-To" Books:

Minilesson: This minilesson is about writing "how-to" books—a sequence of directions for how to do something. One boy offers his writing as a model for the class to discuss the process. (18:52)

Conference with Clementine: The teacher works with Clementine on her how-to book about making an egg carton caterpillar. Clementine revises her piece by adding missing information. The writing piece discussed in this conference is available to print from the DVD under the heading PDF Resources. (7:31)

Conference with Kaya: The teacher works with Kaya on revising her how-to book about making a cake. Kaya works on being more specific in her instructions. (8:17)

Share: The student who shared his writing in the minilesson does so again during the share. The class helps him to determine if any information is missing. (9:39)

Grade 1, Writing Workshop on Adding Important Details:

Minilesson: This minilesson for first graders focuses on how to revise writing by adding important details to help readers understand a story. One child's writing serves as a model. Children are then asked to apply the principle to their own writing during writing workshop. (12:08)

Conference with Isabelle: The teacher confers with Isabelle about adding details to her story. Isabelle determines where the information should go in her piece. (8:33)

Conference with Molly: The teacher works with Molly on how to revise her writing to focus on the most important information for her reader. (12:22)

Conference with Evan: The teacher helps Evan think about revising his writing to include more details for his readers. (8:19)

Share: One student shares her writing as the teacher helps her and the class reflects on the day's minilesson through their feedback. (10:31)

Grade 1, Writing Workshop on Writing Leads:

Minilesson: This minilesson for first graders focuses on how to write a lead for a story. The teacher presents model texts and they discuss why a strong lead is important. Children are asked to read over and revise the leads of their own stories to make sure they engage the reader. (7:59)

Conference with Nicholas: The teacher confers with Nicholas about the lead for a story about his bike. He compares his previous lead with his new one. (4:16)

Conference with John: In this segment, the teacher works with John on a lead for a story about a camping trip. (8:21)

Conference with Morgan: Morgan thinks about what will be most important in her story about Christmas presents. The teacher helps her focus on a small part of her story to help her expand her details. (13:50)

Share: The teacher reiterates the purpose of the lead in a story and has one child read her story to the others. The students' comments help the child to understand what she is communicating in her writing. (8:15)

Grade 2, Writing Workshop on "Show, Don't Tell":

Minilesson: In this minilesson, the teacher helps her second graders learn that writers show their feelings through descriptions rather than simply telling what they are feeling. The teacher uses her own writing as a model. (10:55)

Conference with Anthony, Willy, and Bryn: The teacher confers with three students in a row about applying the minilesson principle to their own writing. (24:09)

Share: Bryn shares her story with the class to illustrate the minilesson principle. The students point out the words she used to show her feelings. (17:28)

PDF Resources

MATERIALS FOR VIEWING TEACHING SEGMENTS

- *Clementine's "How to Make an Egg Carton Caterpillar":* see *Conference with Clementine* on the DVD under Grade 1 Writing Workshop on Writing How-to Books

MATERIALS FOR EXTENSION ACTIVITIES (SEE EXTEND SECTION)

- *Using the Continuum to Assess Student Writing:* This form will help you record your observations and organize your thinking while assessing the writing samples provided.

Writing Samples and Assessments: In this section of the DVD, you will find writing samples for you to analyze using *The Continuum of Literacy Learning, Grades PreK–8* or *PreK–2* as well as completed analyses of each of these samples. These analyses provide insight into how to use the Continuum as a tool to think about what your writers know and what they need to learn more about in the areas of craft, conventions and process.

Note: It is hard to make instructional decisions based solely on one piece of writing. We hope the analyses offered in this section of the DVD will provide you with a process for looking across your students' writing to inform your work within writing workshop. The Extend section below provides details to guide your analysis of these writing samples as well as more in-depth analyses for each grade.

PREKINDERGARTEN

- Water Park—Narrative
- Water Park—Analysis
- Sun and Tree—Functional/Labels
- Sun and Tree—Analysis
- Christmas List—Functional/Lists and Procedures
- Christmas List—Analysis

KINDERGARTEN

- Brady's Birthday—Narrative
- Brady's Birthday—Analysis
- All About Snakes—Informational /Literary Nonfiction
- All About Snakes—Analysis
- Things I Like to Do—Functional/ Lists and Procedures
- Things I Like to Do—Analysis

FIRST GRADE

- Henry's Birthday—Narrative
- Henry's Birthday—Analysis
- Cars—Informational/Literary Nonfiction
- Cars—Analysis
- How to Make a Volcano—Functional/Lists and Procedures
- How to Make a Volcano—Analysis

SECOND GRADE

- The Bat I Killed—Narrative
- The Bat I Killed—Analysis
- Animals—Informational/Literary Nonfiction
- Animals—Analysis

- How to Make Your Own Stamp—Functional/Lists and Procedures
- How to Make Your Own Stamp—Analysis

Preview ▷

If you haven't already, watch the introduction to the Writing continuum on DVD 5 to get an overview of the organization and content of the Writing continuum. Follow the steps in the Preview section of the User Guide for DVD 5 to prepare for your viewing of the lessons on this DVD. If you have already previewed the Writing continuum while using DVD 5, take a moment to review each component of this complex continuum for the grade level featured in the teaching segment(s) you have selected: *Selecting Purpose and Genre* and *Selecting Goals: Behaviors and Understandings to Notice, Teach, and Support* (for **Craft, Conventions,** and **Writing Process**).

Connecting Continua

You may also want to visit the Oral, Visual, and Technological Communication continuum to gain further insight into your observations. Scan the bulleted list of behaviors and understandings for the grade level you have chosen to watch. Notice how you can integrate the goals from more than one continuum into one lesson.

View Without Commentary ▷

After becoming familiar with the different sections of the Writing continuum, view the lesson(s) you have chosen **without commentary** using the suggestions below to focus your observations.

Note: We recommend that you repeat the steps in the next three sections for each of the segments you watch within each classroom's writing workshop. For example, watch the writing minilesson using these steps and then repeat the process for the writing conferences and again for the share. Alternatively, you can watch the entire writing workshop without commentary first, take notes, and then go through the rest of the steps. However, this process may make it hard for you to stay focused and detailed in your study of the observed behaviors and understandings.

 Individual, Small Group & Staff Developers

Record your observations using the following questions to guide your thinking:

- What behaviors are the students demonstrating throughout the minilesson, conference, and/or share? What do they appear to understand about writing?
- What writing behaviors and understandings do you see the teacher supporting or explicitly teaching through the minilesson, conference, and/or share?

Think and/or Discuss ▷

Pause the video segment before watching it with commentary to think about and/or discuss what you observed.

 Individual Study

If you are working alone, review your notes and write down some of the specific behaviors or understandings you noticed as you watched the lesson. Do your best to identify what you have observed.

Small Group Study & Staff Developers

If you are working with a group, discuss what behaviors and understandings you noticed in the lesson with colleagues.

Revisit the Continuum ▷

After you have done your own thinking, open the Writing continuum to the grade level featured in the teaching segment(s) you watched. You may want to focus on one particular aspect of the Writing continuum at a time or scan each section using the guidelines below.

- First, ask yourself whether the lesson you viewed was genre-specific or if it could be applied across genres. If the content of the minilesson, conference, or share was genre-specific, start by reviewing the first section of the Writing continuum, *Selecting a Purpose or Genre.*

    - What genre was featured in the teaching clip you watched?

    - Identify any key understandings under *Understanding the Genre* and *Writing in the Genre* that you saw students demonstrate.

    - Identify the specific key understandings about genre you noticed the teacher teaching for or supporting throughout the teaching interaction.

- Now turn to *Selecting Goals: Behaviors and Understandings to Notice, Teach, and Support* and scan the list of bullets under **Craft** and **Conventions**.

    - Identify the specific bulleted behaviors and understandings you noticed the students demonstrating.

    - Identify the specific bulleted behaviors and understandings you noticed the teacher teaching for or supporting throughout the minilesson, conference, and/or share.

- Now turn to *Selecting Goals: Behaviors and Understandings to Notice, Teach, and Support* and scan the list of bullets under **Writing Process**.

    - Identify the specific bulleted behaviors and understandings you noticed the students demonstrating.

    - Identify the specific bulleted behaviors and understandings you noticed the teacher teaching for or supporting throughout the minilesson, conference, and/or share.

Connecting Continua

You may also want to scan the Oral, Visual, and Technological Communication continuum to gain further insight into your observations. **What behaviors and understandings did you see the students demonstrate or the teacher support from this continuum throughout the teaching segment?**

View With Commentary ▷

Play the video segment **with commentary** and compare what you have observed and discussed with the analysis on the DVD. After you have completed this viewing, think about how you will use what you have learned in your own teaching.

Individual Study

Think about how your new understandings about the Writing continuum and writing workshop will impact your teaching.

- How will what you learned in this section impact your teaching of writing? What will you change tomorrow? What will you change over the course of the next few months?

Small Group Study & Staff Developers

After viewing the clip with commentary, have the group talk about how they will use the Writing continuum in their teaching.

- What have you learned from the lesson(s) you watched and the conversations you have shared that will help you in your teaching?

Extend ▷

After watching these video segments, you may be wondering how these teachers chose to focus on particular behaviors and understandings from the Writing continuum. There are so many components to creating a piece of writing. Where do you begin? The answer lies in your students' writing. Using the continuum as an assessment tool, you can begin to look at your students' writing with new eyes. The continuum helps you identify what your students *understand* about writing and what they *need to understand* about writing or *use more consistently* in their writing.

In this section, you have the opportunity to analyze writing samples from a variety of grades across a variety of genres using the Writing continuum. You can then compare your analysis with the analyses provided on the DVD under PDF Resources. The more detailed analyses offered in this section of the User Guide are designed to help you understand the thinking behind some of the analyses. They also will shed light on how a bulleted behavior/understanding might look when demonstrated in writing as well as how to determine next steps for a writer. We hope this section provides insight into how you might use the continuum in assessing your own students' writing to direct your instruction during writing workshop.

Individual Study

1. If you haven't already, view the PDF Resources available on DVD 6. Either print or view the writing samples that apply to the grade level you are interested in.

   Note: Use the page titled *Dictations and Clarifications of Writing Samples* found in the appendix of this guide to help you understand some of the work of our younger writers. These dictations/translations are a tool for you since you are unable to talk to the students who wrote these pieces directly. We have purposely not included these dictations on the actual samples themselves. (See the *Selecting Purpose and Genre* section of the prekindergarten Writing continuum for more information about dictation.)

2. You may also want to print out the form *Using the Continuum to Assess Student Writing* to help guide your analysis.

3. Read over the writing sample(s) you have selected and do some of your own thinking first before looking at the continuum. Write down the behaviors and understandings you see evident in the writing.

   - What does the writer seem to understand about genre, craft, and conventions? You may want to think about what the student understands about the writing process though it might be difficult to tell in most cases without having seen the writing throughout the process.

   - What are the next steps for this writer? What does he or she need to understand or understand better about writing?

4. Now, turn to the grade level in the Writing continuum for the writing sample you have analyzed. Scan the bullets for each section of the Writing continuum and refine your thinking. What key understandings and behaviors does the writer demonstrate? What bullets would you focus on next with this writer?

5. Compare your own analysis of this writing with those provided on DVD 6 under PDF Resources, Materials for Extension Activities. You will find a detailed analysis for four of the writing samples: Tyler's "Water Park" (PreK); Kyle's "All About Snakes" (K); Alvin's "How to Make a Volcano" (Grade 1); and Adam's "The Bat I Killed" (Grade 2).

6. Lastly, think about the instructional context you might use to teach or support the writer in what he or she needs to learn how to do or do more consistently. As you analyze the writing in your own classroom, you will begin to notice trends. If most of the class seems to be struggling with a particular aspect of writing, you may want to address it during a whole group minilesson. If only one or two students are ready to try a particular aspect of craft, you may want to introduce this in a writing conference or guided writing group versus a whole group minilesson. As you become more familiar with using the Writing continuum as an assessment and planning tool, you will be able to think about how the different instructional contexts of the writing workshop may be used to meet the needs of the writers in your classroom.

 Small Group Study & Staff Developers

If you are working with a group of colleagues, you may want to print out a variety of writing samples found in the PDF Resources section of DVD 6 and divide them among partners in your group. If you are working with a very large group, you can provide packets of these samples and have partners work in groups. Have members of the group follow the same steps described above under the suggestions for individual professional development. Once partners have had the opportunity to analyze the writing, have them share their thinking with the larger group. You can then provide copies of the completed analyses from DVD 6 to generate more discussion and talk about decisions for future instruction.

Analyses of Writing Samples Using the Writing Continuum

The following provides an in-depth analysis of one writing sample from each grade across a variety of genres. Please see the PDF Resources section on this DVD for more writing samples and analyses across grade levels and genres.

PREKINDERGARTEN WRITING

Tyler's one-page narrative piece recalls a memorable event in his life: going to a water park. If we turn to the *Selecting Purpose and Genre* section for the prekindergarten Writing continuum, we can see that Tyler already understands a lot about the narrative genre. (Figure 6.2)

Figure 6.1 Tyler's Writing and Drawing

TYLER	
Understandings About the Genre	**Behavioral Evidence**
▪ You can talk, draw, and write about things that have happened to you	Tyler has used an experience from his own life (going to the water park) for the topic of his story. He has drawn a picture and approximated writing to tell about this experience.
▪ When you talk about or write about something from your own life, you often use the words *I* or *we*	In reading his piece to the teacher, he includes the pronoun *I*. "I went to the water park."
▪ Stories you tell should be interesting to your listeners or readers	Tyler obviously has picked an experience that meant a lot to him and that others might enjoy hearing about. Water parks are exciting places!

Figure 6.2 Tyler's Understandings About the Genre

Tyler's piece also demonstrates his understanding of some of the elements of craft and conventions. (Figures 6.3 and 6.4)

TYLER	
Understandings About Craft	**Behavioral Evidence**
Organization Text Structure: ▪ Use approximated writing and pictures to make short books that tell a story or have information about a topic or theme Presentation of Ideas: ▪ Tell about experiences or topics that can be written by the teacher ▪ Provide some supportive ideas for bigger ideas in talking about a topic or theme	In this one-page story, Tyler attempts to write about his experience going to the water park. When asked to read his story, he responds, "I went to the water park." He appears to label his drawing with the word *me* and has drawn what looks like a water slide, providing some details about his experience. He also appears to approximate the word *sand* with *san* and water with *wr*.
Language Use ▪ What you think you can say, and what you say, you can write	We can tell from his drawing and approximated writing that he understands that you can write about the things you are thinking about.
Voice ▪ Begins to develop interesting ways of talking about personal experiences ▪ Begins to tell stories from a particular perspective	He chose to highlight the water slide in his story of going to the water park. He doesn't draw his car driving there or waiting in line, he has chosen an interesting part to draw to represent the whole experience.

Figure 6.3 Tyler's Understandings About Craft

TYLER	
Understandings About Conventions	**Behavioral Evidence**
Text Layout ■ Begin to understand that print is laid out in certain ways and the lines and spaces are important ■ Begin to write letters and approximated letters in clusters to show the look of words ■ Show awareness of left to right directionality	Tyler appears to be labeling the different parts of his story. We can see he writes *me* on top of the picture of the person and separates the approximated words *san* and *wr* with a space, clearly designating them as two separate words. He is not only approximating words to show the look of words but demonstrates an awareness of left to right directionality as well as some understanding of letter-sound relationships: *san* for *sand* and *wr* for *water*.
Capitalization ■ Understand that there are upper- and lowercase versions of letters	He uses the lowercase *m* and *e* and then, an uppercase *S* and a lowercase *a* and *n* in the word *san*.
Spelling ■ Begin to be aware that a word is always spelled the same	His use of the word *me* demonstrates a beginning understanding of the permanence of words.
Handwriting ■ Begin to understand that writers make decisions about placement of pictures and print	We can tell Tyler intentionally places his print in a way that labels his drawings to explain his idea.

Figure 6.4 Tyler's Understandings About Conventions

Lastly, Tyler has begun to understand features of the writing process. (Figure 6.5)

TYLER	
Understandings About the Writing Process	**Behavioral Evidence**
Rehearsing/Planning Purpose: ■ Draw and write for a specific purpose ■ Choose topics to draw and write about as an individual	Tyler appears to understand he is recounting a personal experience for the enjoyment of others.
Audience: ■ Become aware of the people who will read the writing and what they will want to know ■ Include important information that the audience needs to know	Tyler appears to have a very beginning understanding of audience in his choice of topic. He also labels his drawing in an attempt to communicate important information about his experience.
Drafting/Revising Producing a Draft: ■ Talk about, draw, and approximate writing to produce a piece	Though we don't have insight into how Tyler has talked about his writing, he has demonstrated that he knows how to produce a draft using drawing and approximated writing.

Figure 6.5   Tyler's Understandings About The Writing Process

NEXT STEPS FOR TYLER:

There are many directions the teacher may decide to take in expanding Tyler's understandings about writing. He already demonstrates an understanding of how to choose an interesting topic for his audience and even how to provide a few details about the topic. Building on what he knows about the features of narrative, his teacher might decide to model for him how he can draw a sequence of related pictures and tell about them to expand his ideas. He would probably benefit from interactive and shared writing in which the teacher demonstrates composing a story with a beginning, middle, and end. From this piece of writing, it appears that Tyler is ready to begin thinking about his ideas in a logical sequence, which should be supported through talk first. His teacher might also decide to further develop his voice by demonstrating how to add opinions or feelings to his writing.

Tyler demonstrates an understanding of many of the conventions of writing as described in the prekindergarten continuum. His teacher will want to continue to support his understanding of text layout and directionality through shared and interactive writing. She also may want to show him alternative ways to separate print from pictures to expand his thinking. Lastly, his teacher will want to build upon his understanding of writing approximated words to express his ideas.

In terms of the writing process, Tyler would benefit from talking more about his ideas to expand and add details to his writing during the drafting and planning process. His teacher might also want to demonstrate how to add information and details to his drawings as part of the revising process. This support could be provided through a writing conference or through shared/interactive writing.

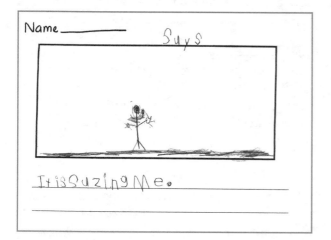

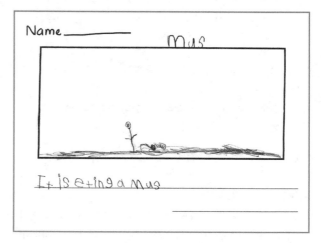

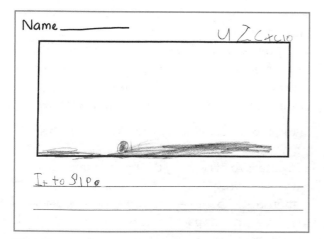

Figure 6.6   Kyle's Writing ,"All About Snakes"

KINDERGARTEN WRITING

"All About Snakes" is an example of a kindergarten piece of informational literary nonfiction (Figure 6.6). It is obvious from this piece of writing that Kyle has seen many examples of literary nonfiction in his classroom and has used these pieces as mentor texts in creating his informational text about snakes.

KYLE	
Understandings About the Genre	**Behavioral Evidence**
■ How to write literary nonfiction from mentor texts ■ Literary nonfiction is writing that engages and entertains readers but teaches them about a topic ■ How to use features (e.g., page numbers, title, labeled pictures, table of contents, others to guide the reader)	Kyle's use of headings on each page not only demonstrates his use of mentor texts in writing this piece but also demonstrates his understanding that headings help guide the reader in informational texts. Kyle demonstrates his understanding of the elements of literary nonfiction as he weaves facts about the snake into his story. For example, his use of the first person on page 2 is entertaining, yet it also teaches the reader about certain snakes' ability to squeeze their prey.

Figure 6.7   Kyle's Understandings About the Genre

Kyle's piece also demonstrates his understanding of some of the elements of craft and conventions as described in the kindergarten continuum (Figures 6.8 and 6.9).

KYLE	
Understanding Abouts Craft	**Behavioral Evidence**
Organization Text Structure: ■ Creates a picture book as one form of writing ■ Includes facts and details in informational writing ■ Puts together the related details on a topic in a text ■ Puts facts or information in order Presentation of Ideas: ■ Tells one idea on each page of a book ■ Presents ideas in a logical sequence Idea Development: ■ Communicates clearly the main points intended for readers to understand	The entire book includes different facts about snakes, demonstrating an understanding of how to put together related details in a text. Kyle also demonstrates a beginning understanding of how to organize these facts into a logical sequence, grouping together the different ways snakes kill their prey and ending with the snake sleeping. He clearly communicates his main points for his readers, including using headings to clarify the contents of the page.
Word Choice ■ Learns new words or phrases from reading and tries them out in writing ■ Uses vocabulary appropriate for the topic	Though we don't know what books have been read in Kyle's classroom, it seems evident that some of his word choices come from research he has done about snakes. His choice of the words "shoots poison" on page 1 and "squeezing" on page 2 seems to come from his reading.
Voice ■ Writes in the way one would speak about a topic ■ States information in a unique or surprising way	Kyle demonstrates a beginning sense of voice as he writes the way he might talk about his topic. His use of the first person on page 2 is a unique or surprising way to present the fact that snakes sometimes constrict their prey.

Figure 6.8   Kyle's Understandings About Craft

KYLE	
Understandings About Conventions	**Behavioral Evidence**
Text Layout ■ Place words in lines, starting left to right, top to bottom ■ Place titles and headings in the appropriate place on a page	This is evident in the way Kyle placed his print.
Grammar Sentence Structure: ■ Use conventional sentence structure (noun + verb) Tense: ■ Write in present tense	With the exception of the last page, Kyle uses conventional sentence structure.
Capitalization ■ Demonstrate knowledge of the use of upper and lowercase letters of the alphabet ■ Use a capital letter for the first word of a sentence	Though Kyle is still working on the formation of his lowercase letters, it is obvious he understands that capital letters start sentences. He begins each sentence with a capital letter and, for the most part, follows with lowercase letters.
Punctuation ■ Use periods as ending marks	With the exception of the sentence on page 4, Kyle consistently uses a period at the end of his sentences.
Spelling ■ Spell high-frequency words *the, it, is, me, a,* and *to* conventionally ■ Attempt unknown words through sound analysis ■ Write some words with consonant letters and consonant clusters (*sn, sh*) appropriate for sounds in the beginning and ending of words ■ Understand that letters represent sounds ■ Construct phonetic spellings that are mostly readable	His approximations of "shoots" with *shoe,* and "sleep" with *slp,* as well as his spelling of "snakes" indicate his beginning understanding of consonant clusters. He needs continued support writing the ending sounds of words as demonstrated by his approximation of "shoot"(*shoe*) and "poison" (*psiss*). He does write the *p* for "sleep" and the *s* at the end of "mouse" but needs to learn to do this more consistently.

Figure 6.9 Kyle's Understandings About Conventions

continues

KYLE	
Kyle's Understanding About Conventions	**Behavioral Evidence**
Handwriting ■ Write letters in groups to form words ■ Write left to right in lines ■ Write letters and words that can be easily read ■ Form upper- and lowercase letters efficiently in manuscript print	Kyle forms many of his upper- and lowercase letters efficiently. He could use support with lower case *p, s,* and *m.*

Figure 6.9 Kyle's Understandings About Conventions *(continued)*

Since we are looking at the final draft for this piece, it is hard to glean all that Kyle might understand about the writing process. For example, we are not privy to what he has done to revise his piece and whether he understands how to add and delete information. However, we are able to infer what he might know about the planning and drafting process (Figure 6.10).

NEXT STEPS FOR KYLE

Kyle has an excellent developing understanding of literary nonfiction. Through further study of this genre, Kyle will be able to grow in his ability to write texts that both teach and entertain. With continued exposure to rich literary nonfiction, he will continue to notice other features of this genre and integrate them into his own crafting of informational literary nonfiction.

Though Kyle's teacher would want to look at multiple pieces of writing to figure out next steps for him as a writer in the areas of craft, conventions, and process, it appears that Kyle would benefit from minilessons and interactive writing lessons demonstrating how to add supporting details to writing. He has a developing sense of how to organize facts and information in an informational text, but could be further sup-

ported in learning how to gather information and put related facts together to expand his writing. In learning how to gather information and add details to his writing, Kyle would increase his knowledge of the writing process, particularly in the area of revision. Specifically, his teacher might begin by demonstrating how to add details to drawings to give more information to the reader and create more opportunities for him to talk about his ideas with teachers and peers. Kyle also appears ready to learn about how to craft a beginning to a story and possibly an ending.

In terms of writing conventions, it appears that Kyle needs to learn to use better spacing between his words to make his message clearer for his readers. He also seems ready to experiment with different ending punctuation (e.g. exclamation points), which would also help him communicate his message to his audience. Kyle is working hard at approximating unknown words through sound analysis. He hears the initial sound of words but only sometimes writes the ending sounds (e.g. *slp* for "sleep," *mus* for "mouse," *shoe psiss* for "shoots poison") of unknown words. Building upon this knowledge, his teacher might choose to support him in listening for and representing ending sounds so that he is able to

KYLE	
Understandings About the Writing Process	**Behavioral Evidence**
Rehearsing/Planning ■ Write for a specific purpose ■ Write to inform readers	Kyle understands that one purpose for writing is to teach his readers about a topic.
Rehearsing/Planning Audience: ■ Think about the people who will read the writing and what they will want to know ■ Include important information that the audience needs to know	Kyle's choice of topics and facts indicates that he has thought about his audience and picked interesting facts to share (e.g. Snakes shoot poison and squeeze their prey.)
Rehearsing/Planning Gathering Seeds/Resources/Experimenting with Writing: ■ Record information in words or drawings Inquiry/Research: ■ Use drawings to tell about a topic	It is clear that Kyle has researched snakes and learned different facts that he is able to put into his own words and communicate to his readers. In addition to his writing, Kyle's drawings provide information about his topic beyond his text. For example, the last page demonstrates that snakes sleep curled up in a ball.
Drafting/Revising Producing a Draft: ■ Use words and drawings to compose and revise text ■ Write a continuous message on a simple topic	It is evident throughout the text that Kyle remains focused on his message of communicating facts about snakes.

Figure 6.10   Kyle's Understandings About the Writing Process

do this more consistently. As Kyle becomes more comfortable with these writing conventions, his teacher may decide to teach him how to check for them in the editing and proofreading part of the writing process. Lastly, as part of his developing understanding of the writing process, Kyle needs to be taught to reread his writing. He most likely would have added the verb on the last page of his writing (*It to slp* for "It goes to sleep") had he reread what he wrote.

GRADE 1 WRITING

"How to Make a Volcano," written by first grader Alvin (Figures 6.11a–e), is a functional piece of writing in the procedural ("how-to") genre. It is clear from Alvin's piece that his class has studied this genre and he has developed some significant understandings about how to write in the genre (Figure 6.12). Please see the Writing continuum for grade 1 as you read this analysis.

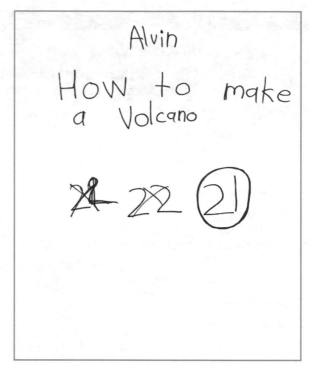

Figure 6.11a   Alvin's Writing, "How to Make a Volcano"

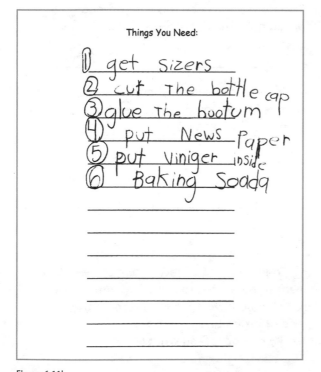

Figure 6.11b

Figure 6.11c

continues

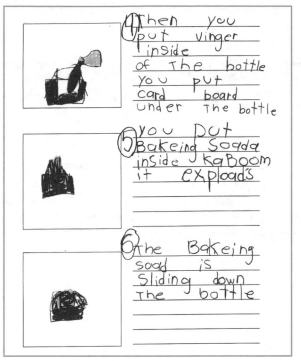

Figure 6.11d

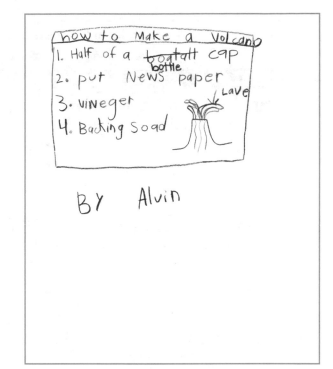

Figure 6.11e

ALVIN	
Understandings About the Genre	**Behavioral Evidence**
<ul><li>The form of a list is usually one item under another and it may be numbered</li><li>Procedural ("how-to") writing as a list of sequential directions for how to do something that also lists what is needed</li><li>Pictures can accompany the writing to help readers understand the information</li></ul>	As we can see from Alvin's diagram on the last page of his work he has a beginning understanding of how to use lists to organize information. He appears to be making a list of the materials needed for his project, but sometimes confuses listing materials with providing sequential directions. Since the paper provides a space for pictures, it is hard to ascertain whether he would add pictures to directions on his own; however, the details he provides in the pictures (e.g. labeling glue) demonstrates that he understands the purpose of the pictures is to further inform readers.

Figure 6.12   Alvin's Understandings About the Genre

Alvin's piece also demonstrates his understanding of some of the elements of craft and conventions as described in the first grade continuum (Figures 6.13 and 6.14).

ALVIN	
Understandings About Craft	**Behavioral Evidence**
Organization Text Structure: ▪ Put together the related details on a topic in a text ▪ Put the information in order ▪ Write a title and the author's name on the cover of a book Beginnings, Endings, Titles: ▪ Select an appropriate title for the piece of writing Presentation of Ideas: ▪ Present ideas in logical sequence Idea Development: ▪ Communicate clearly the main points intended for the reader to understand	Alvin's step-by-step directions and accompanying pictures demonstrate his understanding about how to organize information when writing a procedural piece. His pictures follow the text appropriately and his directions are logical and sequential.
Word Choice ▪ Use vocabulary appropriate for the topic	He uses content-specific words like *volcano*, *baking soda*, and *vinegar* in his writing.
Voice ▪ Write about what is known and remembered ▪ State information in a unique or surprising way	Alvin clearly has done this experiment and is writing from his own experience. His words, "Kaboom, it explodes" demonstrate a sense of voice. It makes his writing unique and surprises the reader with something unexpected in a set of directions.

Figure 6.13 Alvin's Understandings About Craft

ALVIN	
Understandings About Conventions	**Behavioral Evidence**
Text Layout ■ Place words in lines, starting left to right, top to bottom ■ Use spaces between words	This behavior is evident in the visual print.
Grammar Sentence Structure: ■ Use conventional sentence structure (noun + verb) Parts of Speech: ■ Use noun and verb agreement ■ Use prepositional phrases	With the exception of Step 3, Alvin uses conventional sentence structure consistently. Several of the steps contain prepositional phrases (e.g. inside of the bottle; under the bottle).
Capitalization ■ Demonstrate some knowledge of the use of upper- and lowercase letters of the alphabet ■ Show awareness of the first place position of capital letters in words ■ Use uppercase letters in titles	Alvin seems to be developing his understanding of capitalization. He shows some awareness of the first place position of capital letters in words at the beginning of sentences but does not apply these rules consistently.
Spelling ■ Attempt unknown words through sound analysis ■ Use some inflectional endings such as *-s* and *-ing* ■ Represent many short and long vowel sounds in words ■ Represent many consonant sounds or vowel sounds with letters ■ Construct phonetic spellings that are readable ■ Include a vowel in each word ■ Represent consonant blends and digraphs with letter clusters in words	We can see that Alvin is attempting unknown words through sound analysis in his writing of *vinger* and *exploads* for "vinegar" and "explodes." He is still learning about the rules of adding inflectional endings such as *-ing*, but does write them when he hears them (e.g. *bakeing*) He knows that every word needs a vowel and makes sensible attempts using words he knows to approximate unknown words (e.g. *exploads* for "explodes").

Figure 6.14   Alvin's Understandings About Conventions

continues

ALVIN	
Understandings About Conventions	**Behavioral Evidence**
Handwriting ■ Leave appropriate space between words ■ Returns to the left margin to start a new line ■ Write left to right in lines ■ Write letters and words that can be easily read ■ Form upper- and lowercase letters efficiently in manuscript print ■ Form upper- and lowercase letters proportionately in manuscript print	From the directionality and spacing of his print, we know Alvin knows how print works on a page. He will need continued support in keeping his letters on the line and not letting them float above the line.

Figure 6.14 Alvin's Understandings About Conventions *(continued)*

Since we have not been able to observe Alvin as he took this piece through the writing process, we can only make a few inferences about what he knows regarding the writing process (Figure 6.15).

NEXT STEPS FOR ALVIN

Alvin appears to have a strong foundation in the "how-to" genre from the study he has done in his classroom. It will be interesting for his teacher to see if this genre will become a part of his repertoire and if he will select it to fit a particular purpose in the future. Although Alvin understands many things about crafting a piece within this genre, he would benefit from continued support in learning how to expand his details and description to allow someone to follow a sequence of steps. He would benefit from learning more about the revision process and how to use revision tools to add information. Alvin also seems ready to learn about how to write a beginning that would engage the reader. He seems to have

a sense of voice, as we saw in Step 5 of his piece. His teacher may want to build upon his understanding of voice to help him craft a variety of beginnings that would engage the reader.

In terms of conventions, Alvin needs to become more consistent in his application of the rules of capitalization. He appears to have a beginning understanding of when to use uppercase and lowercase letters but needs further support in developing his ability to apply this knowledge consistently. His teacher could provide this support in an individual writing conference, in a small, guided writing group, or in a whole group minilesson depending on the needs of the rest of the class. Lastly, Alvin needs to be taught more about using punctuation at the end of his sentences. In addressing some of these issues, his teacher might also find the opportunity to model the editing and proofreading part of the writing process.

ALVIN	
Understandings About the Writing Process	**Behavioral Evidence**
Rehearsing/Planning Purpose: - Write for a specific purpose - Write name and date on writing	Alvin appears to understand that the purpose of writing a procedural piece is to teach someone how to do something.
Rehearsing/Planning Audience: - Think about the people who will read the writing and what they will want to know - Include important information that the audience needs to know	Alvin picks a topic that he knows might appeal to his peers. He makes sure to include all of the step-by-step directions including an extra diagram box at the end, summarizing what you will need for the experiment.
Rehearsing/Planning Gathering Seeds/Resources/Experimenting With Writing: - Record information in words and/or drawings Inquiry/Research: - Use drawings to tell about a topic Content, Topic, Theme: - Choose topics that one knows about or cares about	Alvin has clearly chosen a topic that he knows about and that he thinks others will find interesting.
Drafting/Revising Producing a Draft: - Use words and drawings to compose and revise text - Write a continuous message on a simple topic	Alvin stays on topic and produces a draft with both words and drawings.

Figure 6.15   Alvin's Understandings About the Writing Process

GRADE 2 WRITING

Adam, a second grader, demonstrates in his piece "The Bat I Killed," his beginning understanding of how to write narrative short fiction (Figures 6.16a–i). Using the second grade continuum, we have analyzed this piece to begin to understand what Adam knows about the genre (Figure 6.17).

Figure 6.16a   Adam's Writing "The Bat I Killed"

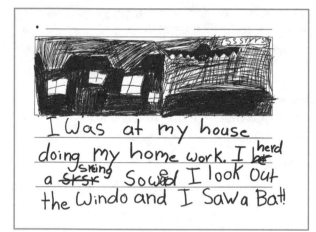

Figure 6.16b

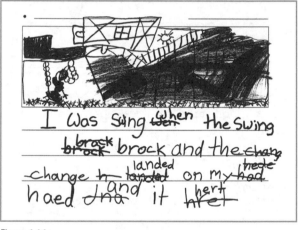

Figure 6.16c

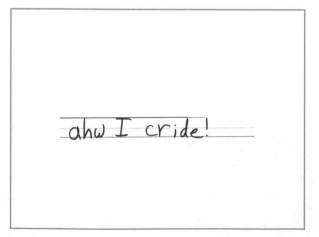

Figure 6.16d

Figure 6.16e

continues

Figure 6.16f

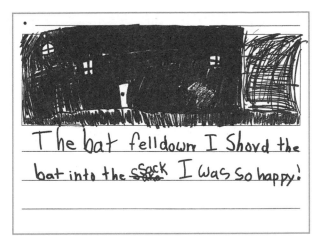

Figure 6.16g

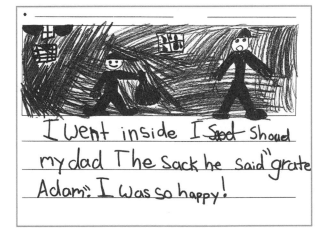

Figure 6.16h

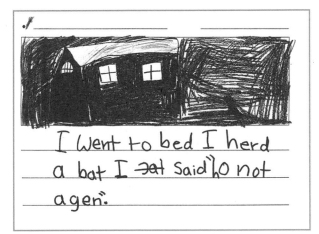

Figure 6.16i

ADAM	
Understandings About the Genre	**Behavioral Evidence**
■ Understand fiction as a short story about an event in the life of a main character ■ Beginning to understand the elements of fiction, including setting, problem, characters, and problem resolution	Adam chose to write about an event (the slaying of a bat) in the life of a character. In this case, he has chosen to write in the first person making the main character himself. He even introduces a second character in the story when he has the dad comment on the killing of the bat. Though he doesn't provide a lot of detail about the setting, he makes sure to tell the reader where the character is in the story (e.g. "I was in my house doing homework; I looked out the window."). He also demonstrates a developing understanding that short fiction often has a text structure that includes a problem and resolution. He establishes that it is a problem having the bat around and resolves it by killing the bat. However, the reader is somewhat unclear why the bat was a problem. From this piece, it would appear that Adam would benefit from reading more about this genre and focusing on how authors in fiction clearly establish the problem for their readers.

Figure 6.17   Adam's Understandings About the Genre

Adam's piece also demonstrates his understanding of some of the elements of craft and conventions as described in the second grade continuum (Figures 6.18 and 6.19).

ADAM	
Understandings About Craft	**Behavioral Evidence**
Organization Text Structure: ■ Write a text that is narrative ordered by time ■ Begin to use underlying structures (problem and solution) ■ Create a picture book as one kind of writing Beginnings, Endings, Titles: ■ Use a variety of endings to engage and satisfy the reader (for example, circular story) ■ Select an appropriate title for a story Presentation of Ideas: ■ Tell one part of the story on each page of the book ■ Present ideas clearly	Adam's text progresses forward in time from when he first sees the bat to when he kills it. As mentioned above, the text demonstrates his developing knowledge of the problem/solution text structure. The bat is the problem (though it is hard to determine exactly why) and the solution is to kill it. Adam's ending demonstrates his understanding of how to craft a circular ending by bringing the bat back into the story at the end. Adam presents his ideas fairly clearly (e.g. "The bat was skreeing I went inside and got a sack I thru the chan and the chan hit the bat…"). The reader gets a fairly clear picture of what has happened in the story. The more Adam learns about the elements of craft, particularly about how to expand important details and omit unnecessary ones, the clearer his writing will become.
Idea Development ■ Communicate main points clearly to readers ■ Provide supporting information or examples that are relevant, and helpful	Adam has a developing understanding of how to communicate the main points of his story clearly to his audience. The reader understands the basic events of the story and most of the details he includes work to develop the story further (e.g. he includes the father's reaction once the bat has been killed, adding emphasis to the fact that a problem has been resolved.) Building on this understanding, Adam will benefit from more instruction in how to evaluate whether the details he includes in a story are relevant and further develop a story or take the reader away from the story.

Figure 6.18   Adam's Understandings About Craft

continues

ADAM	
Understandings About Craft	**Behavioral Evidence**
Word Choice ■ Show ability to vary the text by choosing alternative words	Adam demonstrates his ability to choose interesting words throughout the piece. He uses the word *cried* ("ahw I cride!") instead of *said*. He writes the word *yanked* instead of *pulled* (e.g. "I yankt the chain") and writes "I shovd the bat in the sack" instead of writing, "I *put* the bat into the sack." Not only does he choose alternative words, he selects words that more precisely describe the actions of the character and add to the meaning of the text.
Voice ■ State information in a unique or surprising way ■ Use punctuation to make the text interesting and effective	Adam is developing his voice as a fiction writer. His use of dialogue, word choices, and his clever ending make his piece unique and interesting to read. His use of exclamation points throughout the text demonstrates his beginning understanding of how to communicate meaning through punctuation and make the text interesting to read.

Figure 6.18   Adam's Understandings About Craft *(continued)*

ADAM	
Understandings About Conventions	**Behavioral Evidence**
Text Layout ▪ That layout of print and illustrations is important to conveying the meaning of a text	Adam uses the entire space for his picture allowing him to put in details to support his text. He seems to have a beginning understanding that the layout of the illustrations and print conveys meaning. Notice how the entire background is colored in, creating a more eerie feeling for his bat story.
Grammar Sentence Structure: ▪ Write complete sentences ▪ Use a range of complete sentences (declarative and exclamatory) Parts of Speech: ▪ Use noun and verb agreement ▪ Use prepositional phrases correctly Tense: ▪ Write in past tense	All of Adam's sentences are complete in terms of having a subject and predicate; however, several of his sentences run together. He will need to be taught to identify more consistently complete sentences in order to punctuate them correctly. We can see from the text that he uses both declarative and exclamatory sentences. He matches his nouns and verbs throughout the story and is able to write sentences in the past that include prepositional phrases (e.g. "I shovd the bat into the sack.")
Capitalization ▪ Use a capital letter for the first word of a sentence ▪ Use capitals to start the first letter in the first word, last word, and most other words in title	Adam seems to have some understanding that the first letter of a sentence is capitalized (e.g. "The bat was screeing.") He also knows to capitalize the pronoun *I*. It is difficult to understand if Adam knows how to apply this rule consistently since there are oftentimes two sentences run together. He does not consistently identify complete sentences, which affects his punctuation and therefore, affects his capitalization. He doesn't know the sentence has ended and therefore, does not capitalize in some cases. We also notice that he does not capitalize the word *bat* indicating that he doesn't know the important words in a

Figure 6.19 Adam's Understandings About Conventions

continues

ADAM	
Understandings About Conventions	**Behavioral Evidence**
	title should be in capital letters. He also seems to capitalize sometimes in the middle of sentences. The fact that he mostly writes in lowercase in his sentences indicates that he has some understanding that words in the middle of sentences are not typically capitalized. Therefore, his teacher might want to first prompt for this behavior and if he is not able to self-correct, teach when and why we capitalize words.
Punctuation ■ Use periods and exclamation points as ending marks ■ Use quotation marks around the speaker's exact words	Adam is still learning about punctuation. He uses a range of punctuation in appropriate ways (e.g. exclamation points to convey excitement; quotation marks around some of the speaker's words.) Adam seems to have an understanding that periods and exclamation points are ending marks used to denote the end of a sentence. However, he is very inconsistent in their application. He often does not place a period at the end of complete sentences causing sentences to run together and making it hard for the reader to understand. (e.g., "I went inside I shod my dad The sack he said "grate Adam.") He also has a beginning understanding of how to apply quotations around the speakers' words (e.g. "grate, Adam") However, he does not apply this consistently to all dialogue (e.g, "ahw, I cride!") in the piece.

Figure 6.19   Adam's Understandings About Conventions *(continued)*

continues

ADAM	
Understandings About Conventions	**Behavioral Evidence**
Spelling ■ Correctly spells familiar high-frequency words with regular letter-sound relationships (including consonant blends and digraphs and some vowel patterns), and commonly used endings	Adam spells several high-frequency words correctly and makes several good attempts at words he doesn't know (e.g. *cride, grate*). Adam applies what he knows about long vowels and silent *e* to write these two words. He also demonstrates his ability to hear consonant blends (*sh*) and digraphs (*skr*). Adam seems to need instruction in noticing the way words look in addition to the way they sound. We can tell from his multiple attempts at unknown words that he can identify when a word doesn't look right, but now he needs instruction to help him figure out what would look right. He would also benefit from instruction in how to apply inflectional endings (particularly *-ed*).

Figure 6.19 Adam's Understandings About Conventions *(continued)*

Since we have not been able to observe or talk to Adam as he took this piece through the writing process, we can only make inferences about what he knows regarding the writing process based on his writing (Figure 6.20).

ADAM	
Understandings About the Writing Process	**Behavioral Evidence**
Rehearsing/Planning Purpose: ▪ Write with a specific reader or audience in mind Content, Topic, Theme: ▪ Choose a topic that is significant ▪ Decide what is most important about the story ▪ Stay focused on a topic	It is not clear that Adam has a specific reader in mind as he writes his piece, but it is evident that he understands he must provide background and information for his reader for him or her to understand his story. He includes the setting of the story and explains the problem and resolution so his reader understands what is happening. He also adds dialogue during revision using spider legs, demonstrating that he is thinking about how to make his piece more interesting to his reader. His additions of dialogue also demonstrate that he understands how to change his writing in response to peer and teacher feedback.
Drafting/Revising Understanding the Process: ▪ Change writing in response to peer or teacher feedback Producing a Draft: ▪ Write a draft or discovery draft ▪ Bring the piece to closure with an ending or final statement ▪ Establish an initiating event and follows with a series of events in a narrative Rereading: ▪ Reread and revises the draft or rewrite a section to clarify meaning ▪ Add dialogue to provide information, provide narration or shows thoughts and feelings (in quotes or speech balloons)	Adam understands that producing a draft involves establishing an initiating event (e.g. the bat screeching at his window) and following that with a series of events (how he kills the bat). Adam's clever circular ending demonstrates that he understands this process also involves thinking about how to bring the piece to closure. In order to revise and add dialogue appropriately as he does with the two spider legs (e.g. *ahw, I cride, aw! I was so xuisided*), he had to have reread his writing. He is developing at least a beginning understanding of what it means to read and revise a draft to clarify meaning.

Figure 6.20 Adam's Understandings About the Writing Process

continues

©2011 by Irene Fountas & Gay Su Pinnell

ADAM	
Understandings About the Writing Process	**Behavioral Evidence**
Drafting/Revising Using Tools and Techniques: ■ Use a spider leg or piece of paper taped on to insert text	
Editing and Proofreading Understanding the Process: ■ Understand the writer shows respect to the reader by applying what is known to correct errors ■ Understand that the better the spelling and spacing between words the easier it is for the reader to read it Editing for Conventions: ■ Edit for conventional spelling of important words ■ Edit for spelling of known words ■ Edit for spelling by circling or underlining words that do not look right and making another attempt	It is obvious that Adam makes several attempts to use what he knows to correct the spelling in his piece. He is able to recognize when words don't look right and attempts different spellings, but is not yet able to edit always for conventional spelling. He seems to have a good understanding that it is important to try to make writing as clear as possible for the reader.

Figure 6.20   Adam's Understandings About the Writing Process *(continued)*

NEXT STEPS FOR ADAM

Adam has clearly been exposed to several fictional texts. He has a beginning understanding of how to incorporate the elements of short fiction into his writing, including characters, setting, problem, and solution. He would benefit from further exposure to short fiction texts through interactive read-aloud in which the teacher might help readers think more in depth about one of these elements (e.g., the setting). Adam would also benefit from writing minilessons or small group guided writing lessons demonstrating how to describe a setting when it is important to a story. He also would benefit from learning how to expand important details and omit details that do not move a story along. The teacher again might choose to address this in a whole group setting through writing minilessons, one-on-one in a writing conference, or with a small group in guided writing. Using modeled writing, shared or interactive writing, his teacher could explicitly demonstrate how to revise and focus writing by adding or deleting information.

Adam has a strong voice in his writing, which partially comes from his unique choice of words. He has a large vocabulary, which allows him to choose alternative ways for communicating his ideas. Building upon his descriptive choices of words, his teacher may want to demonstrate how to use his language and vocabulary to show feelings in a story instead of telling them. Throughout "The Bat I Killed," he mentions that the character is excited or happy. Through interactive read-aloud and writing minilessons, his teacher can demonstrate how authors use language to show their readers how characters are feeling so he could integrate this understanding with his strong vocabulary in future writing.

In terms of conventions, Adam seems to need more instruction in how to identify complete sentences. He writes sentences with a subject and predicate but often runs them together, not punctuating with ending marks or noting the beginning of sentences with capitals. His teacher will need to research Adam's writing across several pieces and talk to him about his understanding of capitalization and punctuation in order to determine how she can best instruct him in this area. It is unclear from this piece where his understanding has broken down. Can he identify a complete sentence? Does he know where the sentence ends but does not consistently apply punctuation? Regardless of the specific issue, his teacher will also want to reemphasize why it is important to edit for these conventions. In the end, we want students to care about their readers and show respect to their readers by trying to make their writing as clear as possible.

There are many learning opportunities for Adam as a writer. His teacher will want to choose only a couple of things to address right away with Adam. The goal is for him to learn about writing through the piece he is drafting, revising, and editing and not to perfect the particular piece of writing. Therefore, his teacher will want to look

across several pieces of writing to determine the most valuable next steps for Adam and think about how she can use his current work as a vehicle for learning and practicing those behaviors and understandings.

Give It a Try ▷

 Individual Study

1. Pick three students in your class as case studies to practice using the Continuum as an assessment and planning tool in writing. We recommend picking students of varying levels of understanding to see the different ways the Continuum can help you think about next steps for these writers.

2. Read through a sampling of each of their most recent pieces and go through the steps above for analyzing what the writer knows about craft, conventions, and process. You may want to use the form *Using the Continuum to Assess Student Writing* under PDF Resources to facilitate this process.

3. After determining next steps for each of your students, choose one behavior or understanding you would like to address with this student. Think about how you will provide the support or instruction they need to develop this behavior or understanding as a writer. Determine whether the behavior or understanding you want to address is something the entire class needs (whole group writing minilesson or interactive writing); a topic that only a few children need (a small guided writing group); or something only that child needs or is ready for (individual writing conference).

4. Plan how you will specifically teach for this behavior and understanding and give it a try. See some of the suggestions under Large Group Professional Development to think

about how to plan for these minilessons. Observe each student's current writing to see if this new behavior or understanding is taken on and demonstrated. More importantly, does this behavior and understanding transfer to future writing?

Small Group Study

1. Have each person in the study group bring one or two pieces of writing from one writer in the class to share at your next small group meeting.

2. In partners, have teachers work together to analyze the writing using the Continuum for evidence of what the student understands about craft, conventions, and process. You may want to use the form *Using the Continuum to Assess Student Writing* under PDF Resources to facilitate this process.

3. With the same partners, ask them to plan a writing minilesson to address one of the behaviors/understandings for which this writer might need instruction. See some of the suggestions under Large Group Professional Development to think about how to plan for these minilessons.

4. Ask the groups to go back to their classrooms and teach the lesson inbetween meeting times.

5. For the next meeting, ask your colleagues to bring examples of student writing and reflect on how the students applied the new learning. Talk about continued next steps for these students.

6. Discuss how you can use this process to look at the rest of the students in your class. Help your colleagues develop a feasible plan for continually assessing student writing and planning based on their understandings and need for growth as writers.

Large Group Facilitator

1. If you have the opportunity, ask participants to bring a sample of student writing to analyze within small groups. We recommend working in partners to assess the writing. If participants are unable to bring student writing, provide them with student writing from PDF Resources on DVD 6 to use instead.

2. Analyze the students' writing for craft, conventions, and process as demonstrated above. You can use the form *Using the Continuum to Assess Student Writing* to facilitate your thinking.

3. After determining next steps, ask participants to plan a writing minilesson to address one of the behaviors/understandings for which the student needs support or instruction. Have them work with a partner to develop a writing minilesson to address this behavior or understanding. Provide participants with the following questions to guide their thinking.

   ■ Think about the bullet you have chosen to address in the writing minilesson. Unpack this bullet by thinking about all it encompasses. Ask yourself what your student would need to be able to do to really demonstrate this behavior or understanding.

   ■ Can this be addressed in one minilesson or should it be the subject of a series of minilessons?

   ■ If you determine it would be taught over a series of minilessons, what would that look like? Develop a minilesson statement for the overreaching goal and minilessons for each successive lesson. For example:

   Bullet from Grade 1 Continuum:

   Craft, Organization, Idea Development: Provide supportive description, details or examples to explain the important ideas.

To demonstrate this behavior, students must be able to identify the important ideas in their story and think about the kinds of details that would support these ideas. We have provided an example below of an overarching minilesson statement and some subsequent minilessons that would in essence create a unit of study around this bulleted behavior.

Overarching Writing Minilesson Statement:

Writers provide descriptions and details in their stories to explain the important ideas to their readers.

Possibilities for subsequent minilesson statements on adding description and detail:

- Writers ask themselves what the most important ideas are in their stories to make them clear to their readers. (This lesson would focus on teaching writers to identify their most important ideas. We need to make sure they actually can identify the central points of their writing before we ask them to add more detail.)

- Writers make their writing clearer by adding details and descriptions in several ways.

- Writers sometimes describe the details of an event in the story to make their ideas clearer to their readers.

- Writers sometimes describe the setting of their story to make their story clearer to their readers.

- Writers sometimes describe the characters in their story to make the story clearer to their readers.

Note: There are any number of minilessons that might follow from this idea but this example is meant to get you thinking how these bullets might translate into instruction.

- If you determine the bullet you have chosen could be addressed in one minilesson, think about if there are other bullets connected to this behavior and understanding that could be grouped together to create a unit of study. How would you group these together?

4. Have partners share their ideas with the rest of the people at their table. Discuss how this process of assessing and planning using the Continuum will impact their teaching.

©2011 by Irene Fountas & Gay Su Pinnell

DVD 7

Phonics, Spelling, and Word Study

On DVD 7, you will see examples of how teachers use the Phonics, Spelling, and Word Study continuum to help children learn important principles for how words "work," so that they can solve words while reading, and spell them accurately while writing.

The introduction to the DVD provides an overview of the Phonics, Spelling, and Word Study continuum which is organized according to the nine areas of learning described in Fountas and Pinnell's *Phonics Lessons: Letters, Words, and How They Work,* for kindergarten, grade one, grade two, and grade three. You will also find the nine areas defined in the introduction to the Phonics, Spelling, and Word Study section of the continuum. These areas include: (1) early literacy concepts; (2) phonological awareness; (3) letter knowledge; (4) letter-sound relationships; (5) spelling patterns; (6) high-frequency words; (7) word meaning and vocabulary; (8) word structure; and (9) word-solving actions. Several of the teaching segments on this DVD focus on this last area of the continuum—teaching word-solving actions. This area is the most important component of the Phonics, Spelling, and Word Study continuum because it requires readers and writers to use all of the other eight categories mentioned above in an applied way while reading and writing.

In addition, the DVD introduction references other resources to help you in planning phonics, spelling, and word study instruction in your classroom, including the detailed Phonics continuum and monthly planner from *Phonics Lessons* or *Word Study Lessons: Letters, Words, and How They Work*, published by Heinemann. This continuum is also included at the end of *The Continuum of Literacy Learning, Grades PreK–8*.

Before beginning your study of this continuum, play the introduction to DVD 7 and read the introductory materials related to the Phonics, Spelling, and Word Study continuum in *The Continuum of Literacy Learning, Grades PreK–8* or *PreK–2*.

Research ▷

You can find more information about the nine areas of learning for phonics, spelling, and word study in the following resources:

Phonics Lessons: Letters, Words, and How They Work, Grades K–2 (Pinnell and Fountas, Heinemann, 2002). This text provides information about the complex, intricate relationships between letters and sounds and the ways in which they work to support developing readers. In addition to a monthly planner, this series comes with over 100 minilessons per grade.

Word Matters: Teaching Phonics and Spelling in the Reading/Writing Classroom (Pinnell and Fountas, Heinemann, 1998). This text provides information on designing and implementing a systematic approach for helping children learn about letters, sounds, and words with a focus on helping children become word solvers in both reading and writing. It provides theoretical underpinnings as well as practical suggestions for setting up word study in your classroom.

Other chapters in our texts that will help you develop your understanding of the nine areas of learning for phonics, spelling, and word study are:

When Readers Struggle: Teaching That Works (Pinnell and Fountas, Heinemann, 2009)

- Chapter 8: "Words Matter: Building Power in Vocabulary"
- Chapter 9: "The Phonological Base for Learning to Read and Write"
- Chapter 10: "Learning About Print: Early Reading Behaviors"
- Chapter 11: "Learning to Solve Words: Effective and Efficient Phonics"

- Chapter 12: "Building and Using a Repertoire of Words"

Guiding Readers and Writers: Teaching Comprehension, Genre, and Content Literacy (Fountas and Pinnell, Heinemann, 2001) (particularly for grade 2 and up)

- Chapter 3: "Investigating and Using Language: The Language and Word Study Design"
- Chapter 22: "Teaching for Word Solving: Phonics, Spelling, and Vocabulary"

Guided Reading: Good First Teaching for All Children (Fountas and Pinnell, Heinemann, 1996)

- Chapter 13: "Learning About Letters and Words"

For more information about how to integrate word work into interactive writing lessons:

Interactive Writing: How Language and Literacy Come Together, K–2 (McCarrier, Pinnell, and Fountas, Heinemann, 1999)

- Chapter 7: "Constructing a Text: Learning About Letters and How Print Works"
- Chapter 8: "Constructing a Text: Learning How Words Work"

Select a Clip and Print Supporting Materials ▷

Select teaching segments from the DVD that are close to your grade level(s) of interest. There are no PDF Resources available on DVD 7. The activities for extending your learning of the Phonics, Spelling, and Word Study continuum utilize some of the PDF Resources available on DVD 6. Read the Extend section below to determine whether you will need these materials.

Video Segment Descriptions and Running Times

Prekindergarten, Name Chart: The teacher works with a group of prekindergarten children, helping them notice features of their names. They use the name chart to make connections between the first letters in their names and other words. (1:11)

Prekindergarten, Name Puzzles: In this segment, prekindergarten children learn how to use name puzzles. They put the letters of their names together to form the word and then check it carefully. (4:06)

Prekindergarten, Magnet Letters: The teacher works with a small group of prekindergarten children to notice the features of letters. They sort magnetic letters into groups—those with circles and those with lines. (4:23)

Grade 1, Word Parts: In this segment children are learning to take words apart using the onset and rime. (14:42)

Grade 1, Plurals: In this segment the teacher presents a phonics/word study minilesson on plurals. The teacher uses simple, known words as her examples. Children work with magnetic letters to physically add an *s* to a word. They then use the word in a sentence. (16:36)

Grade 1, Word Endings: These first-grade children work on adding –*ed* endings to words. They work with words they know and learn that the ending has several sounds. (10:52)

Grade 1, Contractions: In this lesson, grade one children work with examples of *am*, *is* and *will* contractions. They play the game "Concentration" matching contractions with the two words they represent. (20:29)

Grade 2, Silent Consonants: The teacher helps his second-grade students understand which words have silent consonants. The teacher and the students offer examples of such words in given categories. (9:36)

Grade 2, Letter-Sound Relationships: The teacher in this lesson helps students notice and use the onset and rime in one-syllable words to help read, write, and spell them. (7:48)

PDF Resources

The supporting materials for the Phonics, Spelling, and Word Study continuum are available under PDF Resources on **DVD 6: Writing: Focus on Writing Workshop,** and can be used to extend your understanding of the Phonics, Spelling, and Word Study continuum. To determine which supporting materials to print, read the Extend section below. If you plan to expand your study as suggested in this section, print the following writing samples from DVD 6:

- Water Park—Prekindergarten (Narrative)
- Things I Like to Do—Kindergarten (Functional)
- Henry's Birthday—Grade 1 (Narrative)
- Animals—Grade 2 (Informational)

Preview ▷

Before viewing the teaching segment, scan the bulleted behaviors and understandings listed under the nine categories of learning for the Phonics, Spelling, and Word Study continuum for the grade level of the teaching segment you have selected.

View Without Commentary

 Individual, Small Group & Staff Developers

View the lessons you have chosen **without commentary**. Take notes using the following suggestions to guide your observations:

- Identify behaviors and understandings you observe in the children's talk. What behaviors and understandings do they seem to control?

- Identify the behaviors and understandings explicitly taught or prompted by the teacher.

- Identify behaviors and understandings that might be the focus of future teaching.

Think and/or Discuss ▷

Pause the video segment before watching it with commentary to think about and/or discuss what you observed.

 Individual Study

If you are working alone, review your notes and write down some of the specific behaviors or understandings you may have noticed as you watched the lesson. Do your best to name what you have observed.

 Small Group & Large Group

If you are working with a group, discuss what behaviors and understandings you noticed in the lesson with colleagues.

Revisit the Continuum ▷

 Individual , Small Group & Staff Developers

After you have done your own thinking, reopen the continuum to the section you viewed earlier.

- Identify the specific bulleted behaviors and understandings you noticed the students demonstrating.

- Identify the specific bulleted behaviors and understandings you noticed the teacher teaching for or supporting throughout the lesson.

- Identify the specific bulleted behaviors and understandings you see as areas for future reading.

View With Commentary ▷

Now play the video segment **with commentary** and compare what you have observed and discussed with the analysis on the DVD.

 Individual Study

Think about how your new understandings about the Phonics, Spelling, and Word Study continuum will impact your teaching.

- How will what you learned in this section impact your teaching of word study? Reading? Writing?

- What will you change tomorrow? What will you change over the course of the next few months?

 Small Group & Large Group

After viewing the clip with commentary, have the group talk about how they will use the Phonics, Spelling, and Word Study continuum in their teaching.

- What have you learned from the lesson(s) you watched and the conversations you have shared that will help you in your teaching of word study, reading, and writing?

Extend ▷

The Phonics, Spelling, and Word Study continuum can also be used as a tool for looking at student writing to determine what the child knows about the way words "work" and what they need to still learn about the principles of word study.

1. Print out the following writing sample(s) that pertains to your grade level of interest from the PDF Resources section of **DVD 6: Writing: Focus on Writing Workshop.**

    Note: Dictations and translations for student writing samples are available in the appendix of this guide.)

    - Water Park—Prekindergarten (Narrative)

    - Things I Like to Do—Kindergarten (Functional)

    - Henry's Birthday—Grade 1 (Narrative)

    - Animals—Grade 2 (Informational)

2. Turn to the grade level in the Phonics, Spelling, and Word Study continuum that applies to the piece of writing you have selected. Analyze the piece of writing with the following questions in mind:

    - What does the student demonstrate he or she understands about the way words work?

    - Determine some next steps for this child in learning about phonics, spelling, and word study.

Note: In your own classroom, you would want to look across several pieces of writing to determine next steps for your students.)

 Individual Study

If you are working alone, compare your thinking with the analyses below.

 Small Group & Large Group

If you are working in a group, discuss your thinking with a partner and then share with the whole group. Remember writing is only one source of information in determining what students know about the way words work. You will want to look across instructional contexts to determine how to best support word solvers in your classroom.

Figure 7.1 Tyler's Writing, "Water Park"

Water Park—Prekindergarten (Narrative)
Analysis of Writing Using the Phonics, Spelling, and Word Study Continuum

Areas of Phonics, Spelling, and Word Study Continuum	Behaviors and Understandings Evidenced in Writing (from the Continuum, PreK)	Possible Behaviors and Understandings to Teach or Support in Instruction
Early Literacy Concepts	■ Understands that print conveys meaning ■ Distinguishes between print and pictures ■ Understands the concept of word ■ Uses left to right directionality	
Phonological Awareness	■ Understands that words are made up of sounds	■ Clap the syllables of words with teacher help ■ Say onsets and rimes of words with teacher help
Letter Knowledge	■ Notices that letters have different shapes ■ Understands the concept of a letter ■ Understands that words are made up of letters ■ Produces approximated writing ■ Uses approximated writing functionally (labels) ■ Begins to use efficient and consistent motions to form letters	
Letter-Sound Relationships	■ Understands that there is a relationship between letters and the sounds in words	■ Say words slowly as part of shared/interactive writing

Figure 7.2 Analysis of Writing, "Water Park"

continues

Water Park—Prekindergarten (Narrative)
Analysis of Writing Using the Phonics, Spelling, and Word Study Continuum

Areas of Phonics, Spelling, and Word Study Continuum	Behaviors and Understandings Evidenced in Writing (from the Continuum, PreK)	Possible Behaviors and Understandings to Teach or Support in Instruction
Word Meaning	N/A	■ Notice and use new and interesting words heard in texts read and in conversation
Spelling Patterns	Not demonstrated in this piece	■ Recognize that there are patterns in words that you can hear and say
High-Frequency Words	■ Recognizes a few high-frequency words after experience in shared and interactive writing (e.g. *me*)	
Word Structure	■ Understands that words can have more than one part that you can hear (e.g. *wr* for *water*)	■ Clap words to show awareness of syllables
Word-Solving Actions	■ Uses own name and other known words as a resource in approximated writing (e.g. Tyler may have used the last part of his name to hear the last sound in the word *water—wr*)	■ Recognize and locate a few high-frequency words ■ Make connections between own name and other words ■ Use own name and other known words as a resource in approximated writing

Figure 7.2 Analysis of Writing, "Water Park" *(continued)*

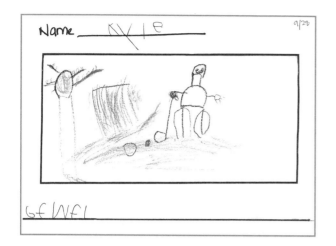

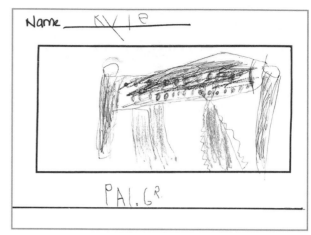

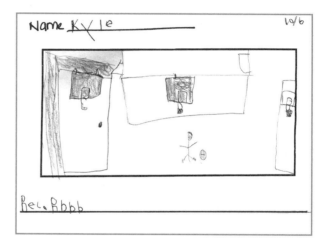

Figure 7.3   Kyle's Writing, "Things I Like to Do"

Things I Like to Do—Kindergarten (Functional)
Analysis of Writing Using the Phonics, Spelling, and Word Study Continuum

Areas of Phonics, Spelling, and Word Study Continuum	Behaviors and Understandings Evidenced in Writing (from the Continuum, PreK)	Possible Behaviors and Understandings to Teach or Support in Instruction
Early Literacy Concepts	■ Distinguishes between print and pictures ■ Understands the purpose of print in writing ■ Recognizes one's name ■ Understands the concepts of letter and word ■ Uses left-to-right directionality of print ■ Uses spaces between words when writing (beginning)	■ Use space between words when writing more consistently ■ Understand the concept of a sentence as a group of words with ending punctuation
Phonological Awareness	■ Hears and recognizes word boundaries (e.g. places a space between words and even sometimes incorrectly places a period between words, designating these boundaries) ■ Hears and says beginning phonemes (sounds) in words and ending (inconsistently)	■ Segment sentences into words ■ Segment words into phonemes ■ Hear and say beginning phonemes (sounds) in words and ending—needs support, particularly in hearing and writing ending sounds ■ Hear and say syllables
Letter Knowledge	■ Uses efficient and consistent motions to form letters when writing	■ Make connections between words by recognizing letters, letter clusters and letter sequences

Figure 7.4 Analysis of Writing, "Things I Like to Do"

continues

Things I Like to Do—Kindergarten (Functional)
Analysis of Writing Using the Phonics, Spelling, and Word Study Continuum

Areas of Phonics, Spelling, and Word Study Continuum	Behaviors and Understandings Evidenced in Writing (from the Continuum, PreK)	Possible Behaviors and Understandings to Teach or Support in Instruction
Letter-Sound Relationships	■ Recognizes and uses beginning consonant sounds and the letters that represent them to read and write words ■ Understands that there is a relationship between sounds and letters ■ Attempts to write words by writing one letter for each sound heard.	■ Attempt to write words by writing one letter for each sound heard. (Kyle demonstrates a beginning understanding of how to do this, but would benefit from continued modeling and instruction in this area, perhaps through interactive writing)
Spelling Patterns	Not demonstrated in this piece	■ Recognize and use a few simple phonograms with a vowel/consonant pattern
High-Frequency Words	Not demonstrated in this piece	■ Write a core of twenty to twenty-five high-frequency words
Word Meaning	Not demonstrated in this piece	
Word Structure	N/A	
Word-Solving Actions	■ Uses letters and relationships to sounds to read and write words	■ Use known words to help in spelling new words ■ Recognize and spell known words quickly

Figure 7.4 Analysis of Writing, "Things I Like to Do" *(continued)*

Haley 9/20   Henry's Birthday

I went to my frend
Henry's Birthday and
We Jumpt Jumpt
In a Moon Bouns
He is 3

9/27

My Mom cailed us for
ca kac canke We
came

9/27

then we sat doun and
Sanzg Happy Birthday
to him   the ...

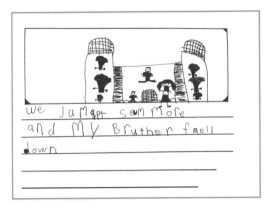

We Jumpet sam more
and My Bruther faell
down

10/5

We did Presens
Me and My brather
got him a Jat truuk
truuk

then Henry got us
our guay a bag he ser
BY Haley and James
I Whavde BY

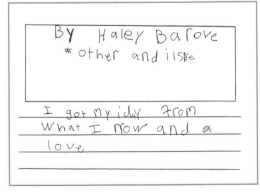

BY Haley Barove
other and ilsre

I got my idy from
what I now and a
love

Figure 7.5 Haley's Writing, "Henry's Birthday"

Henry's Birthday—Grade 1 (Narrative)
Analysis of Writing Using the Phonics, Spelling, and Word Study Continuum

Areas of Phonics, Spelling, and Word Study Continuum	Behaviors and Understandings Evidenced in Writing (from the Continuum, PreK)	Possible Behaviors and Understandings to Teach or Support in Instruction
Early Literacy Concepts	▪ Understands the concept of letter and word ▪ Uses left to right directionality of print and returns to left in writing ▪ Uses spaces between words when writing ▪ Matches one spoken word to one written word while writing	▪ Understand the concept of a sentence as a group of words with ending punctuation. (Haley has a beginning understanding of the concept of a sentence, but does not use ending punctuation in her writing.)
Phonological Awareness	▪ Segments sentences into words ▪ Hears and recognizes word boundaries ▪ Hears and says beginning phonemes in words and ending	▪ Segment words into phonemes (She seems to have a beginning understanding of how to do this but might benefit from more instruction in this area to help with her spelling.)
Letter Knowledge	▪ Uses efficient and consistent motions to form letters when writing	▪ Make connections between words by recognizing letters, letter clusters and letter sequences
Letter-Sound Relationships	▪ Recognizes and uses beginning consonant sounds and the letters that represent them to read and write words ▪ Recognizes that letter clusters (blends and digraphs) represent consonant sounds	

Figure 7.6   Analysis of Writing, "Henry's Birthday" *(continued)*

continues

©2011 by Irene Fountas & Gay Su Pinnell

Henry's Birthday—Grade 1 (Narrative)
Analysis of Writing Using the Phonics, Spelling, and Word Study Continuum

Areas of Phonics, Spelling, and Word Study Continuum	Behaviors and Understandings Evidenced in Writing (from the Continuum, PreK)	Possible Behaviors and Understandings to Teach or Support in Instruction
Letter-Sound Relationships, *cont.*	■ Hears and identifies long and short vowel sounds in words and the letters that represent them (e.g. *cake, truck*) ■ Recognizes and uses other vowel sounds (*oo* as in *moon; ou* as in *bounce*)	■ Recognize and use other vowel sounds (Haley has a beginning understanding but needs more support and instruction in different vowel sounds.)
Spelling Patterns	■ Recognizes and uses a large number of phonograms (VC, CVC, CVC, VCC) ■ Recognizes that words have letter patterns that are connected to sounds (phonograms and other letter patterns)	■ Recognizes that words have letter patterns that are connected to sounds (phonograms and other letter patterns). (Haley demonstrates a beginning understanding of the connection between sounds and different letter patterns but could use continued instruction in this area.)
High-Frequency Words	■ Writes a core of at least fifty high-frequency words	■ She would benefit from continued support in developing her base of high-frequency words.
Word Meaning	Not demonstrated in this piece	■ Recognize and use simple homophones (e.g. *by/bye*)

Figure 7.6 Analysis of Writing, "Henry's Birthday" *(continued)*

continues

Henry's Birthday—Grade 1 (Narrative)
Analysis of Writing Using the Phonics, Spelling, and Word Study Continuum

Areas of Phonics, Spelling, and Word Study Continuum	Behaviors and Understandings Evidenced in Writing (from the Continuum, PreK)	Possible Behaviors and Understandings to Teach or Support in Instruction
Word Structure	**Syllables** ■ Understands how vowels appear in syllables (each of her syllables has a vowel) **Plurals** ■ Has beginning understanding of the concept of plurals and plural forms: adding –s **Verb Endings** ■ Recognizes and uses endings that add –ed to a verb to make it past tense (inconsistently) **Possessives** ■ Recognizes and uses possessives that add an apostrophe and an s to a singular noun	**Plurals** ■ Understand the concept of adding -es to words ending in *x, ch, sh, s, ss, tch, zz* (It is not clear from the writing if she has an understanding of this concept but since she is already using plurals, it might be a good place to start) **Verb Endings** ■ Recognize and use endings that add –ed to a verb to make it past tense (Haley does this inconsistently—adding -ed to *called* but writing *jumpt* for *jumped*; she needs to understand that *ed* sometimes makes a *t* sound at the end of words.)
Word-Solving Actions	■ Uses letters and relationships to sounds to write words	■ Use known words and word parts to help in spelling new words ■ Change onset or rime to make a new word (It is difficult to ascertain from the writing if she is already doing this, but it will certainly help her increase her spelling power if she learns how.)

Figure 7.6   Analysis of Writing, "Henry's Birthday" *(continued)*

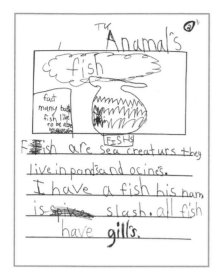

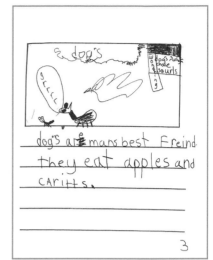

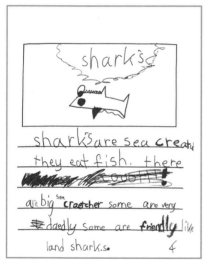

Figure 7.7   Student Writing, "Animals"

Animals—Grade 2 (Informational)
Analysis of Writing Using the Phonics, Spelling, and Word Study Continuum

Areas of Phonics, Spelling, and Word Study Continuum	Behaviors and Understandings Evidenced in Writing (from the Continuum, PreK)	Possible Behaviors and Understandings to Teach or Support in Instruction
Letter-Sound Relationships	■ Recognizes and uses the full range of consonant letters and letter clusters (*st, ch*) in the beginning, middle, and ending position in words ■ Recognizes and uses long and short vowel sounds in words ■ Recognizes and uses letter combinations that represent long vowel sounds (e.g. *creatures*) ■ Recognizes and uses vowel sounds in open syllables (e.g. CV: *wa-ter*) ■ Recognizes and uses vowel sounds in closed syllables (eg. CVC *tur-tle*) ■ Recognizes and uses vowel sounds with *r* (e.g. *turtles, sharks*)	■ Recognize and use letter combinations that represent long vowel sounds (Ty has a beginning understanding that long vowel sounds can be represented in different ways but could probably use more support in developing this concept.)
Spelling Patterns	■ Recognizes and uses a large number of phonograms	■ Recognizes and uses a large number of phonograms (Though he uses a variety of phonograms in his writing, he will need continued instruction in this area to continue to grow.

Figure 7.8 Analysis of Writing, "Animals"

continues

Animals—Grade 2 (Informational)
Analysis of Writing Using the Phonics, Spelling, and Word Study Continuum

Areas of Phonics, Spelling, and Word Study Continuum	Behaviors and Understandings Evidenced in Writing (from the Continuum, PreK)	Possible Behaviors and Understandings to Teach or Support in Instruction
High-Frequency Words	■ Writes several high-frequency words automatically (*are, they, very, eat, some, big*, etc.)	■ Employ self-monitoring strategies for continually accumulating ability to write accurately a large core of high-frequency words (working toward automatic knowledge of the five hundred most frequent)
Word Meaning	Not demonstrated in this piece	(Since Ty does not use many compound words, synonyms, antonyms or homophones in this piece, it is hard to infer what instruction he needs in this area. His teacher would want to look across his writing to see evidence of his understanding of word meaning.)
Word Structure	Syllables ■ Understands how vowels appear in syllables (every syllable has a vowel) Base Words ■ Removes the ending from a base word to make a new word (e.g. *friend, friendly*—he seems to understand this idea though he reverses the vowels when he writes the base word)	Syllables ■ Recognize and use syllables in words with double consonants (e.g. *car-rot* vs. *caritt*) Plurals ■ Understand the concept of plurals and plural forms: adding *–s*; adding *–es*; and changing spelling (Ty is clearly confusing plurals and possessives and will need instruction in learning how to apply each appropriately.)

Figure 7.8 Analysis of Writing, "Animals" *(continued)*

continues

Animals—Grade 2 (Informational)		
Analysis of Writing Using the Phonics, Spelling, and Word Study Continuum		
Areas of Phonics, Spelling, and Word Study Continuum	**Behaviors and Understandings Evidenced in Writing (from the Continuum, PreK)**	**Possible Behaviors and Understandings to Teach or Support in Instruction**
Word Structure, *cont.*		Possessives ■ Recognize and use possessives that add an apostrophe and an *s* to a singular noun
Word-Solving Actions	■ Uses letters and relationships to sounds to write words	■ Use known words to monitor spelling (Ty is inconsistent, often writing words in different ways throughout his piece. His teacher will need to investigate this further. Does he not really know the word or is he not self-monitoring? (e.g. *friend, friendly*) ■ Use known words and word parts to help in spelling new words ■ Notice patterns and categorize high-frequency words to assist in learning them quickly ■ Recognize base words and remove prefixes and suffixes to break them down and solve them

Figure 7.8 Analysis of Writing, "Animals" *(continued)*

Give It a Try ▷

Individual Study

1. Collect writing samples and reading records of three of the students in your classroom. Try to choose students of varying levels of understanding across the Phonics, Spelling, and Word Study continuum.

2. Analyze these different sources of information to figure out what each student understands about the way words work. In which areas do they need the most support? Plan a word study lesson to address one of these needs.

3. Think about how you will differentiate word study in your classroom to meet these varying needs.

4. How will this knowledge impact your instruction in reading and writing?

  Small Group & Large Group

1. Ask colleagues to bring a writing sample and reading record of one of the students in their class.

2. With partners, use the Continuum to analyze the writing and reading record for evidence of what the student knows about the way words work and what he or she needs to learn.

3. Share your findings with the whole group or at tables and discuss how this knowledge will impact your instruction in word study, reading, and writing.

DVD 8

Guided Reading

Guided reading allows you to differentiate literacy instruction in your classroom through small group, targeted instruction. This targeted instruction provides individual readers with the support they need to read increasingly challenging texts, giving them the tools to grow as independent readers. Though students need plenty of time to read independently to practice and enjoy processing a variety of texts, they also need to be a part of guided instruction, which supports them in further developing a flexible and efficient processing system. Guided reading is based on authentic, on-going assessment, which allows teachers to differentiate instruction to meet the needs of similar readers. By bringing together small, dynamic groups of readers who are reading at nearly the same level, you are able to more efficiently meet the needs of several children at once. The Guided Reading continuum addresses the two critical pieces of information you need to know in planning guided reading: what demands a text will place on readers, and what behaviors and understandings your readers bring to the reading experience. Knowing these two sources of information will help you figure out what books to match to readers and in what ways you can support those readers so they can learn more.

You will notice the Guided Reading continuum is organized by text level rather than grade level. This will help you in selecting texts that are at your students' varying instructional levels. The Guided Reading continuum is based on the Fountas and Pinnell A to Z text gradient™ which is designed as a tool for teachers to use in selecting books for readers. You can find the text gradient, as well as the grade level expectations for reading by level, in Figure 8.1. To determine each student's instructional reading level, you can use Fountas and Pinnell's *Benchmark Assessment System,* which correlates directly to the A to Z levels of the Guided Reading continuum. To learn more about this system, visit www.fountasandpinnell.com.

DVD 8 focuses on how to use the Guided Reading continuum as both an assessment and planning tool for small group instruction of reading. The User Guide and DVD will demonstrate how to analyze text characteristics to determine the demands of a text on your readers, as well as help you think about the ways readers are expected to think within, beyond, and about texts at increasingly challenging text levels. Using the continuum as a tool to analyze reading behaviors will help you understand

©2011 by Irene Fountas & Gay Su Pinnell

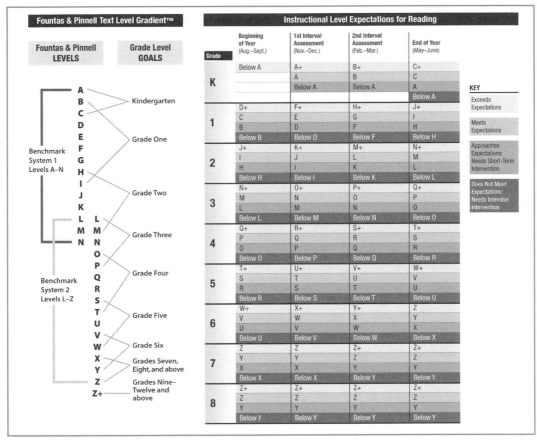

Figure 8.1   Fountas & Pinnell Text Level Gradient™ and Instructional Level Expectations for Reading

where your readers are and where you want to take them. The suggested activities for viewing the DVD as well as the commentary for each video clip will help you hone your ability to observe reading behaviors and notice how different teachers support their readers in thinking within, beyond, and about a text throughout the guided reading lesson. **The section on Assessment on DVD 1 provides more insight into how to analyze the behaviors of readers using the continuum. This in-depth study of how to use the continuum for assessment in reading is essential to the planning and teaching of guided reading. If you have yet to explore DVD 1, we suggest you begin your study there before viewing DVD 8: Guided Reading.**

To begin exploring guided reading, **play the introduction to DVD 8,** which provides an overview of the structure of a guided reading lesson and a brief introduction to the gradient of texts.

Research ▷

In the introduction to DVD 8, as well as in the introductory materials to the Guided Reading continuum in *The Continuum of Literacy Learning, Grades PreK–8* and *PreK–2,* you will find a description of the simple structure of a guided reading lesson. Though the DVD will provide examples of guided reading lessons, the purpose of this DVD is to help you refine your instruction within guided reading using the Guided Reading continuum. The introductory matter to the Guided Reading continuum in *The Continuum of Literacy Learning, Grades PreK–8* and *PreK–2* provides some background information about the components of a guided reading lesson. However, if you would like more information about the structure and elements of a guided reading, as well as the logistics of managing guided reading, read or revisit some of the texts suggested below.

Before viewing the video segments, you may also want to try a few guided reading lessons on your own if you are not using guided reading on an ongoing basis in your classroom. Familiarizing yourself with the procedures and routines of guided reading before viewing the video segments will allow you to focus more on the reading behaviors demonstrated by the students and supported and taught by the teachers in the teaching segments.

Besides understanding the structure of a guided reading lesson, you will want to have a strong foundation in understanding the systems of strategic actions for processing written texts before exploring guided reading. The introductory materials to the Guided Reading continuum in *The Continuum of Literacy Learning, Grades PreK–8* and *PreK–2* provide some helpful background on the subject, but the texts listed below offer an opportunity for more in-depth study of the reading process.

Teaching for Comprehending and Fluency (Fountas and Pinnell, Heinemann, 2006)

- Chapter 24: "Using Guided Reading to Teach Comprehending and Fluency"

- Chapter 25: "Using Guided Reading to Teach for the Comprehending of Fiction Texts"

- Chapter 26: "Using Guided Reading to Teach for the Comprehending of Nonfiction Texts"

Guiding Reading: Good First Teaching for All Children (Fountas and Pinnell, Heinemann, 1996)

This text provides an introduction to the essentials of guided reading, including managing the classroom while pulling small groups, understanding the text gradient and leveled books, using running records, and forming dynamic guided reading groups.

Guiding Readers and Writers (Fountas and Pinnell, Heinemann, 2001)

Note: Though this text focuses on examples from the intermediate grades, it provides information about the components of a guided reading lesson, teaching for strategic actions, and how to select and introduce texts that apply to all grades.

- Chapter 11: "Understanding Guided Reading"

- Chapter 12: "Planning for Guided Reading"

- Chapter 13: "Dynamic Grouping for Effective Teaching in Guided Reading"

- Chapter 14: "Selecting, Introducing, and Using Leveled Texts"

- Chapter 20: "Teaching for Sustaining Strategies in Guided Reading"

- Chapter 21: "Teaching for Connecting and Expanding Strategies in Guided Reading"

Select a Clip and Print Supporting Materials ▷

Select a video segment that is close to the text levels you are interested in and print any of the needed supporting materials described below.

Video Segment Descriptions and Running Times

Level C, *Clean My Teeth*: The teacher provides a supportive introduction to this level C text as she points out some of the vocabulary and challenging language structure. Among other things, children learn to use a known word to monitor their reading. (15:41)

Level F, *Tim's Favorite Toy*: A first grade group reading a level F fiction book first discusses the idea of favorite toys. The teacher uses the language of the text in her introduction of it. After reading the text, the children discuss cause and effect. (15:23)

Level G, *Locked Out*: This group of first graders is reads a level G fiction book. They discuss personal experiences with being locked out of their homes and work on fluency. (28:16)

Level G, *How Animals Move*: The teacher helps first graders to notice how the writer has organized the text. After reading, the students discuss some of the new information they encountered. The teacher helps them to realize that they can look at the parts of longer words in order to solve them. (24:29)

Level K, *Lions and Tigers*: This first-grade group reads a level K nonfiction book about lions and tigers, and the teacher introduces them to some of the technical words they will encounter during the reading. They also go over the structure of this informational text and focus on plurals during word work. (35:53)

Level K, *Classroom Pets*: In this first grade group, the kids read a level K book about pets that are appropriate to have in classrooms. They make predictions about the animals they will encounter in the book and what makes them good classroom pets. The teacher also helps them understand the different meanings of homophones. (36:29)

Level K, *Emergency Vehicles*: This first-grade group is reading a level K nonfiction text about different kinds of emergency vehicles. The teacher introduces the different types of emergencies that the book details. They use the introduction of the book to get an overview before reading on their own and use the table of contents and graphic features to understand the text. (25:49)

Level K, *Frog and Toad Are Friends*: This second grade group is reading a fiction story with familiar characters. They work on reading with expression and making sure their reading makes sense. After reading, they discuss the turning point in the story. (33:28)

PDF Resources

MATERIALS FOR VIEWING TEACHING SEGMENTS

- Text Analysis of *Clean My Teeth* (Level C)

- Text Analysis of *Tim's Favorite Toy* (Level F)

- Text Analysis of *Locked Out* (Level G)

- Text Analysis of *How Animals Move* (Level G)

- Text Analysis of *Lions and Tigers* (Level K)

- Text Analysis of *Classroom Pets* (Level K)

- Text Analysis of *Emergency Vehicles* (Level K)
- Text Analysis of *Frog and Toad Are Friends* (Level K)
- Observing Guided Reading Note-taking Form

MATERIALS FOR EXTENDING UNDERSTANDING (SEE EXTEND SECTION)

- Text Analysis Form

Preview ▷

Before beginning each segment, preview the *Selecting Texts* and *Selecting Goals* section for the level of the text featured in the teaching segment you have chosen to view. As part of your preview of the text characteristics for each level, you will find text analyses below for each book featured on this DVD. These are also printable from your DVD under PDF Resources.

Selecting Texts

Text selection is an essential part of guided reading. Consider several factors while selecting books for your students including their background experience, their interests and the supports and demands offered by the text. Choose texts that engage your students, are at their instructional level and offer opportunities for learning and problem solving.

 Individual Study

To begin your preparations for viewing the teaching segment you have selected:

- Turn to the corresponding level in the Guided Reading continuum for the text level featured in the video segment.

- Begin by reading the brief description of the characteristics of readers who can generally read the types of texts found at this level. Of course, readers are individuals and vary widely but this description provides some general expectations for readers reading texts at this level. This section will help you think about your readers as you form guided reading groups and try to select appropriate instructional texts.

- Next, scan the characteristics of texts at this level. You will notice that these text characteristics are organized into ten categories in the same way as the other reading continua. As with readers, there is a great variety of texts at each level. Though the text characteristics apply to what is generally true for texts at this level, it is important to analyze texts individually for the demands they will place on your readers. The text analyses below demonstrate that some factors will apply to some texts and not to others at the same level. Understanding the demands of a text and knowing what your readers are able to do will inform how you introduce the text and support your readers in processing it.

- Take a moment now to scan the text analysis for the text featured in the clip(s) you have selected to watch (see Figures 8.2 through 8.9). Think about which characteristics might be supportive for readers at this level and which might place demands on them. If you don't have students reading at this instructional level in your classroom, use the description of readers in this section to hypothesize what might be demanding for readers at this level.

 Small Group Study & Staff Developers

If you are working with a group, you may want to pass around all of the text analyses and talk about the apparent supports and demands of each of these texts. As you talk about each one, think specifically about students you know. You may notice that though many challenges will be the same for readers at this level, there will be some variation for individuals.

Text Analysis: *Clean My Teeth*

Text Factor	Analysis
Genre and Form	■ Simple animal fantasy ■ Form: Picture Book
Text Structure	■ Simple narrative with several repetitive episodes
Content	■ Accessible content (animals) ■ Most concepts supported by illustrations except for the main problem (It is not obvious that the crocodile wants his teeth cleaned from the picture)
Themes and Ideas	■ Concrete, easy to understand idea ■ Familiar theme (animals are afraid of a bigger, scarier animal)
Language and Literary Features	■ Amusing, one-dimensional characters ■ Repeating natural language patterns ■ Simple dialogue (assigned by *said*) ■ Told in third person ■ Element of fantasy (talking animals) ■ Speech bubbles contain the same language as the text ■ Solution to story is only found in speech bubble
Sentence Complexity	■ Simple, predictable sentence structure with little variation (alternates putting *said* before or after dialogue) ■ Last sentence breaks from the repetition by adding the word *please* ■ All sentences are part of dialogue with the subject and predicate alternating places
Vocabulary	■ Most vocabulary familiar to children and likely to be used in their oral language ■ Content-specific words illustrated in the text

Figure 8.2 Text Analysis of *Clean My Teeth*

continues

Text Analysis: *Clean My Teeth*

Text Factor	Analysis
Words	<ul><li>All one- to two-syllable words</li><li>Mostly simple plurals except for *stories*</li><li>Many high-frequency words</li><li>Mostly one-syllable words (except for *crocodile)*</li><li>Some words used in different language structures ("Crocodile said," "said Snake")</li><li>Variety of easy spelling patterns</li></ul>
Illustrations	<ul><li>Illustrations match print closely</li><li>Illustrations on every page</li><li>Some meaning is carried in the text and less with picture support (concept of crocodile asking for his teeth to be cleaned)</li><li>Consistent layout of illustrations and print</li></ul>
Book and Print Features	Length:<ul><li>13 pages</li><li>One to two lines of text per page</li></ul>Print and Layout:<ul><li>Print in large plain font</li><li>Ample spacing between words and lines</li><li>Sentences turn over one line in the same way across multiple pages</li><li>Consistent placement of print</li><li>Line breaks match ends of phrases and sentences</li><li>Speech bubbles on every page repeating what is in the text</li><li>A Rebus story at the end</li></ul>Punctuation:<ul><li>Periods</li><li>Exclamation points</li><li>Commas</li><li>Quotation marks</li></ul>

Figure 8.2   Text Analysis of *Clean My Teeth (continued)*

Text Analysis: *Tim's Favorite Toy*

Text Factor	Analysis
Genre and Form	■ Realistic Fiction ■ Form: Picture Book
Text Structure	■ Narrative text with clear beginning, series of events, and ending
Content	■ Familiar content (school) ■ Concepts accessible through text and illustrations (children bringing different toys to school)
Themes and Ideas	■ Theme related to typical experiences of children (toy day in school) ■ Concrete, easy-to-understand ideas
Language and Literary Features	■ Amusing and engaging one-dimensional characters ■ Text with familiar school setting close to children's experiences ■ Both simple and split dialogue, speaker usually assigned ■ Some longer stretches of dialogue (one 6 lines long) ■ Simple sequence of events (repeated with children showing the class their favorite toys)
Sentence Complexity	■ Some long sentences (more than ten words) with prepositional phrases, adjectives, and clauses ("Yes Michael," said Mrs. Hill, "and after that, we will look at the dinosaurs, teddy bears, and dolls.") ■ Some sentences that are questions in simple sentences and in dialogue ("Can I show my fire engine to the children now?") ■ Sentences with prepositional phrases and adjectives ■ Variation in placement of subject, verb, adjectives, and adverbs ■ Use of commas to set words apart ■ Some compound sentences conjoined by *and*
Vocabulary	■ Most vocabulary words familiar to children and likely to be used in their oral language

Figure 8.3 Text Analysis of *Tim's Favorite Toy*

continues

Text Analysis: *Tim's Favorite Toy*

Text Factor	Analysis
Words	■ Mostly one- to two-syllable words ■ Some three-syllable words (*dinosaur, favorite*) ■ Plurals and possessives ■ Many high-frequency words ■ Some words with inflectional endings (*laughed, looked, showed, dinosaurs, toys*) ■ Mostly words with easy predictable letter-sound relationships and spelling patterns ■ Some complex letter-sound relationships in words (*dinosaurs, engine, laughed*) ■ Some words used multiple times in different language structures (*said*) ■ Variety of easy spelling patterns
Illustrations	■ Highly supportive illustrations that match the text ■ Illustrations that support the text but do not carry all important aspects of meaning ■ More details in the illustrations
Book and Print Features	Length: ■ Sixteen pages of print ■ Longest page of text has eight lines of print Print and Layout: ■ Ample space between words and lines ■ Print in large, plain font ■ Some words in bold for emphasis ■ Some sentences carrying over two to three lines ■ Except for the first two pages, all of the print is on the left-hand page ■ Print is clearly separated from pictures ■ Text with layout that supports phrasing Punctuation: ■ Periods, commas, quotation marks, question marks, and exclamation marks

Figure 8.3 Text Analysis of *Tim's Favorite Toy (continued)*

Text Analysis: *Locked Out*

Text Factor	Analysis
Genre and Form	■ Realistic Fiction ■ Form: Picture Book
Text Structure	■ Narrative plot ■ Series of episodes ■ Straightforward problem and solution
Content	■ Accessible, familiar content (getting locked out) ■ Concepts accessible through text and illustrations
Themes and Ideas	■ Theme is related to typical experiences of children ■ Another related theme (child helping parent) ■ Concrete, easy-to-understand ideas
Language and Literary Features	■ Told in third person ■ Simple, assigned dialogue with some split dialogue and longer stretches of dialogue ■ Simple sequence of events
Sentence Complexity	■ Mostly simple sentences; longer ones connected by simple conjunctions like *and* ■ Sentences are short but some contain prepositional phrases ■ Some sentences are questions in simple sentences and in dialogue
Vocabulary	■ Most vocabulary familiar to children and likely to be used in their oral language ■ Some content-specific words illustrated in the text (*flowerpots, shed*)

Figure 8.4 Text Analysis of *Locked Out*

continues

Text Analysis: *Locked Out*

Text Factor	Analysis
Words	■ Many high-frequency words ■ Mostly one- or two-syllable words ■ A few compound words ■ Easy contractions ■ Variety of easy spelling patterns ■ Some words used multiple times in different language structures ("mom said," "said mom")
Illustrations	■ Illustrations support and extend meaning but do not carry all of the important information in the print ■ Illustrations on every page ■ A few illustrations are more complex and require reader to infer the feelings of the character from the drawing
Book and Print Features	Length: ■ 16 pages ■ 3-8 lines of text per page Print and Layout: ■ Print in large plain font ■ Ample spacing between words and lines ■ Some words in bold ■ Wrapping sentences on two or three lines but always on the same page ■ Print is clearly separated from the pictures ■ All sentences start on left margin Punctuation: ■ Periods ■ Exclamation points ■ Commas ■ Quotation marks ■ Question marks

Figure 8.4   Text Analysis of *Locked Out (continued)*

Text Analysis: *How Animals Move*

Text Factor	Analysis
Genre and Form	■ Informational Text ■ Form: Picture Book
Text Structure	■ Focused on a single topic (movement) ■ Repeated text structure (*This _____ can ____.*) ■ Largely focused on one category of information (how animals move) ■ Longer text with repeating, more complex pattern which follows a simple pattern ■ Unusual format with one question followed by the answer; text ends with a question that requires an answer
Content	■ Accessible content that expands beyond home, neighborhood, and school ■ Concepts accessible through text and illustrations
Themes and Ideas	■ Concrete, easy-to-understand ideas
Language and Literary Features	■ Simple sequence of repeated events (how different animals and people move)
Sentence Complexity	■ Two long sentences (11 words in length) with prepositional phrases and adjectives ■ Two questions
Vocabulary	■ Most vocabulary words familiar to children and likely to be used in their oral language ■ Some content-specific words introduced and illustrated in the text (*manatee, flippers, leopard*)

continues

Figure 8.5   Text Analysis of *How Animals Move*

Text Analysis: *How Animals Move*

Text Factor	Analysis
Words	■ Mostly one- to two-syllable words ■ Some three-syllable words (*animals, kangaroo, manatee*) ■ Many high-frequency words ■ Some complex letter-sound relationships in words (*people, leopard, move, climb*) ■ Wide variety of easy spelling patterns (*run, hop, fly, can*)
Illustrations	■ Illustrations that support and extend meaning but do not carry all of the important information in the print ■ Illustrations on every page
Book and Print Features	Length: ■ Sixteen pages of print ■ One to three lines of print per page Print and Layout: ■ Ample space between words and lines ■ One word in all caps for emphasis (YOU) ■ Sentences carrying over two lines ■ Print is clearly separated from the pictures ■ Layout of print supports phrasing Punctuation: ■ Periods, ellipses, commas, and question marks

Figure 8.5   Text Analysis of *How Animals Move (continued)*

Text Analysis: *Lions and Tigers*

Text Factor	Analysis
Genre and Form	▪ Informational Text ▪ Form: Picture Book
Text Structure	▪ Presentation of multiple topics (African lions, lionesses and their cubs, Asian tigers and tiger cubs) ▪ Text organized into a few simple categories ▪ Variety in nonfiction formats (questions and answers in boxed arrows on most pages)
Content	▪ Familiar content and some new content that typically children would not know (a pride, the countries and continents where the animals live) ▪ New content requiring prior knowledge to understand (map of North and South America, Africa and Asia) ▪ Text with setting outside children's typical experience ▪ New content accessible through text and illustrations
Themes and Ideas	▪ Some ideas new to most children (habitats of lions and tigers and how they hunt and live) ▪ Themes (topics) accessible given typical experiences of children (lions and tigers) ▪ Text with universal themes illustrating important human issues (taking care of the young)
Language and Literary Features	▪ Text with settings that are not typical of many children's experiences (the wild in North and South America, Africa, and Asia) ▪ Text told from a single point of view
Sentence Complexity	▪ Variety in sentence length and complexity ▪ Longer (more than fifteen words), more complex sentences (prepositional phrases, introductory clauses) ▪ Many complex sentences with embedded phrases and clauses ▪ Variation in placement of subject, verb, adjectives and adverbs

Figure 8.6 Text Analysis of *Lions and Tigers*

continues

Text Analysis: *Lions and Tigers*

Text Factor	Analysis
Vocabulary	■ Content words illustrated with pictures (*mane, lioness, pride, tigress, cubs*) ■ Some new vocabulary and content-specific words introduced, explained, and illustrated in the text
Words	■ Many two- to three-syllable words ■ Plurals, contractions, and possessives (*lion's, lionesses*) ■ A wide range of high-frequency words ■ Some words with inflectional endings (*easiest, bigger, biggest*) ■ A few words with complex letter-sound relationships ■ A few words with complex spelling patterns (*beautiful, easiest, each, lionesses*) ■ Multisyllable words that are challenging to take apart or decode (*beautiful, together, easiest, toward*) ■ Some easy compound words (*sometimes, cannot, themselves*)
Illustrations	■ Some long stretches of text with no illustrations or graphics ■ Variety in the layout of print (question in boxed arrow with answer in boxed arrow on next page)
Book and Print Features	Length: ■ Sixteen pages ■ Many lines of print on each page (up to 14 lines) Print and Layout: ■ Ample space between lines ■ Print and font size vary with the boxed print in smaller font ■ Use of words in bold to indicate emphasis and level of importance ■ Variety in background color ■ Sentences carrying over two to five lines ■ Print and illustrations are integrated Punctuation: ■ Periods, commas, question marks, apostrophes, and dashes. Tools: ■ Table of contents, index, headings

Figure 8.6 Text Analysis of *Lions and Tigers (continued)*

Text Analysis: *Classroom Pets*

Text Factor	Analysis
Genre and Form	▪ Informational Text ▪ Form: Picture Book
Text Structure	▪ Presentation of multiple topics (guinea pig, gerbil, tarantula, leopard gecko, and red-eared slider turtle) ▪ Text is ordered into a few simple categories of classroom pets ▪ Variety in organization (narrative, bulleted list of things to do, numbered list of how to create a home for a classroom pet) ▪ Variety in nonfiction formats (see above)
Content	▪ Familiar content and some new content that typically children would not know ▪ New content requiring prior knowledge to understand (reptiles and rodents) ▪ New content accessible through text and illustrations
Themes and Ideas	▪ Some ideas might be new to most children (how to care for a gerbil, tarantula shedding its skin, gecko can't make its own body heat) ▪ Theme accessible given typical experiences of children (care of classroom pets) ▪ Text with universal theme illustrating important human issues and attributes (care of living things)
Language and Literary Features	▪ Text told from a single point of view
Sentence Complexity	▪ Variety in sentence length and complexity ▪ Longer (more than fifteen words), more complex sentences (prepositional phrases, introductory clauses and lists of nouns) ▪ Many complex sentences with embedded phrases ▪ Variation in placement of subject, verb, adjectives, and adverbs
Vocabulary	▪ Content words illustrated with pictures (*rodent, pellets, vitamins, reptiles*) ▪ Some new vocabulary and content-specific words introduced, explained, and illustrated in the text (*leopard gecko, red-eared slider turtle, pellets*)

Figure 8.7 Text Analysis of *Classroom Pets*

continues

Text Analysis: *Classroom Pets*

Text Factor	Analysis
Words	▪ Many two- to three-syllable words ▪ Plurals, contractions, and possessives (*let's, it's, don't, won't, pets, crickets, reptiles, its*) ▪ A wide range of high-frequency words ▪ Many words with inflectional endings (*putting, cupping, handling, spotted*) ▪ Many words with complex letter-sound relationships (*guinea, special*) ▪ Some complex spelling patterns (*guinea, vegetables, areas, fruit, red-eared*) ▪ Multisyllable words that are challenging to take apart or decode (*vegetables*) ▪ Easy compound words (*classroom*) ▪ Hyphenated words (*red-eared, cold-blooded*)
Illustrations	▪ Some long stretches of text with no illustrations or graphics ▪ Variety of layout of print (narrative, bulleted and numbered lists)
Book and Print Features	Length: ▪ Sixteen pages ▪ Many lines of print on a page (four to fifteen lines) Print and Layout: ▪ Ample space between lines ▪ Print and font size vary with some longer texts in smaller fonts ▪ Use of words in bold and different colored print and background to indicate emphasis and titles of a section ▪ Variety in print and background color ▪ Sentences carrying over two to four lines ▪ Print and illustrations integrated Punctuation: ▪ Question marks, commas, periods, apostrophes, hyphens Tools: ▪ Table of contents, glossary, and headings

Figure 8.7 Text Analysis of *Classroom Pets (continued)*

Text Analysis: *Emergency Vehicles*

Text Factor	Analysis
Genre and Form	▪ Informational Text ▪ Form: Picture Book
Text Structure	▪ Underlying structure (description) ▪ Text organized into simple categories (ten different emergency vehicles) ▪ Variety in organization and topic (one list of things to do if there is a fire at home, one letter from a woman explaining why she needed a snow ambulance) ▪ Variety in format (letter, lists, boxes that give important facts about the topic)
Content	▪ Familiar content and some new content that typically children would not know ▪ Some settings outside children's typical experience ▪ Potentially new content accessible through text and illustrations (snow ambulance, air ambulance, police boats)
Themes and Ideas	▪ Some ideas new to most children ▪ Theme accessible given typical experiences of children (emergency vehicles)
Language and Literary Features	▪ Some text with settings that are not typical of many children's experiences ▪ Told from a single point of view
Sentence Complexity	▪ Variety in sentence length and complexity ▪ Longer (more than fifteen words), more complex sentences (prepositional phrases, introductory clauses, list of verbs) ▪ Some complex sentences with embedded phrases and clauses ▪ Variation in placement of subject, verb, adjectives, and adverbs
Vocabulary	▪ Content words illustrated with pictures or other graphics ▪ Some new vocabulary and content-specific words introduced, explained, and illustrated in the text (*fire hydrant, siren, vehicle, emergency*)

Figure 8.8 Text Analysis of *Emergency Vehicles*

continues

Text Analysis: *Emergency Vehicles*

Text Factor	Analysis
Words	■ Many two- to three-syllable words ■ Plurals and one contraction (*don't*) ■ A wide range of high-frequency words ■ Some words with inflectional endings ■ Some words with complex letter-sound relationships (*buildings, hydrants, firefighters*) ■ Some complex spelling patterns ■ Multisyllable words that are challenging to take apart or decode ■ One easy compound word (*firefighters*)
Illustrations	■ Variety in the layout of print (e.g. boxes with facts, a letter, and a list of what to do if there is a fire at home)
Book and Print Features	Length: ■ Many lines of print on a page (2 to 11 lines) Print and Layout: ■ Ample space between lines ■ Print and font size vary (handwriting in the letter, red letters for emphasis) ■ Sentences carrying over two to three lines Punctuation: ■ Periods, commas, question marks, exclamation marks, dashes Tools: ■ Questions at the end of the book ■ Glossary ■ Index ■ Table of contents

Figure 8.8 Text Analysis of *Emergency Vehicles (continued)*

Text Analysis: *Frog and Toad Are Friends*

Text Factor	Analysis
Genre and Form	■ Simple Animal Fantasy ■ Form: Beginning chapter book with illustrations
Text Structure	■ Narrative with many episodes ■ Short chapters ■ Chapters connected by characters ■ Simple, straightforward plots
Content	■ Some plots and situations outside typical experience ■ New content accessible through text and illustrations
Themes and Ideas	■ Many light, humorous stories typical of childhood experiences ■ Text with universal theme illustrating important human issues and attributes (friendship, best friends)
Language and Literary Features	■ Memorable characters ■ Setting important to understanding the plot in the text ■ Text told from a single point of view
Sentence Complexity	■ Variety in sentence length and complexity ■ Longer (more than fifteen words), more complex sentences ■ Many complex sentences with embedded phrases and clauses (prepositional phrases, introductory clauses, lists of nouns, verbs, or adjectives) ■ Many complex sentences with embedded phrases and clauses ■ Variation in placement of subject, verb, adjectives, and adverbs ■ Wide variety of words to assign dialogue, with verbs and adverbs essential to meaning
Vocabulary	■ Content words illustrated with pictures (*raccoon, calendar, buttons*) ■ Some new vocabulary and content-specific words introduced, explained, and illustrated in the text (*bathing suit, sparrow, riverbank*) ■ Wide variety of words to assign dialogue, with verbs and adverbs essential to meaning (*screamed, cried, shouted, asked*)

Figure 8.9   Text Analysis of *Frog and Toad Are Friends*

continues

Text Analysis: *Frog and Toad Are Friends*

Text Factor	Analysis
Words	■ Many two- to three-syllable words ■ Plurals, contractions, and possessives ■ A wide range of high-frequency words ■ Many words with inflectional endings (*fallen, climbed, banging*) ■ Many words with complex letter-sound relationships (*thought, meadow, hurried, laughing*) ■ Some complex spelling patterns (*calendar, thought, laughing, against, raccoon*) ■ Multisyllable words that are challenging to take apart or decode (*crawled, beautiful, envelope, knocked, sewing*) ■ Some easy compound words (*into, mailbox*)
Illustrations	■ Some long stretches of text with no illustrations ■ Illustrations support interpretation, enhance enjoyment, and set the mood but are not necessary for understanding
Book and Print Features	Length: ■ Sixty-four pages Print and Layout: ■ Ample space between lines ■ Use of words in italics and all capitals to indicate emphasis or signal other meaning ■ Variety of print color in table of contents and chapter headings ■ Sentences carrying over two to three lines ■ Print and illustrations integrated ■ Usually friendly layout in chapter books, with many sentences starting on the left Punctuation: ■ Periods, commas, quotation marks, exclamation points, question marks Tools: ■ Readers' tools (table of contents and chapter titles)

Figure 8.9   Text Analysis of *Frog and Toad Are Friends (continued)*

Selecting Goals

The section for *Selecting Goals: Behaviors to Notice, Teach, and Support* is the heart of the Guided Reading continuum. It provides a description of the expectations for thinking on the part of readers at this level. Turn to the level that corresponds to the text featured in the teaching segment you have selected to watch. As you scan the list of behaviors, you will notice they are organized into the categories for **thinking within, beyond, and about text,** and then further divided into twelve subcategories representing the **systems for strategic actions**. You can use this section to guide your assessment and planning for every part of a guided reading lesson:

- Planning the introduction to texts
- Guiding interactions with individual readers
- Discussing the meaning of text after reading the whole text or part of it
- Making specific teaching points after reading
- Planning for word work
- Planning ways to extend the understanding of the text

The introductory materials to the Guided Reading continuum in *The Continuum of Literacy Learning, Grades PreK-8* and *PreK-2,* as well as each teaching segment on DVD 8, provide more insight into how to use the Guided Reading continuum in each part of the guided reading lesson. Familiarizing yourself with the bullets in the *Selecting Goals* section before watching the teaching clips you have selected will help you identify the behaviors the students are demonstrating and those the teacher is supporting throughout the lesson.

View Without Commentary ▷

  Individual, Small Group & Staff Developers

As you watch each section of the guided reading lesson without commentary, record the **behaviors and understandings** you notice the students demonstrating and those you see the teacher supporting through explicit teaching and prompting throughout the lesson. To facilitate your observations, you may want to use the note-taking form titled *Observing Guided Reading* found under PDF Resources on the DVD.

  Small Group & Large Group

If you are working with colleagues, we recommend pausing after each part of the guided reading lesson (e.g. introduction, reading the text, discussing the text) to discuss what you have observed.

Think and/or Discuss ▷

Pause the video segment before watching it with commentary to think about and/or discuss what you observed.

 Individual Study

If you are working alone, review your notes and write down some of the specific behaviors or understandings you may have noticed as you watched the lesson. Do your best to name what you have observed.

Small Group & Large Group

If you are working with a group, discuss what behaviors and understandings you noticed in the lesson with colleagues. As suggested above, it may be helpful to pause after each part of the guided reading lesson to discuss what you have observed instead of discussing the whole lesson at one time.

Revisit the Continuum ▷

   Individual, Small Group & Staff Developers

After you have done your own thinking, reopen the continuum to the section you viewed earlier.

- Identify the specific bulleted behaviors and understandings you noticed the students demonstrating.

- Identify the specific bulleted behaviors and understandings you noticed the teacher teaching for or supporting throughout the lesson.

- Identify the specific bulleted behaviors and understandings you see as areas for future reading.

View With Commentary ▷

Now play the video segment **with commentary** and compare what you have observed and discussed with the analysis on the DVD. After you have completed this viewing, think about how you will use what you have learned in your own teaching.

 Individual Study

Think about how your new understandings about the Guided Reading continuum will impact your teaching.

- How will what you learned in this section impact your teaching of reading? What will you change tomorrow? What will you change over the course of the next few months?

  Small Group Study & Staff Developers

After viewing the clip with commentary, have the group talk about how they will use the Guided Reading continuum in their teaching.

- What have you learned from the lesson(s) you watched and the conversations you have shared that will help you in your teaching?

Extend ▷

This section will give you an opportunity to think more deeply about how to use the Guided Reading continuum as a planning tool and how to translate the bulleted behaviors and understandings into instruction using *Prompting Guide, Part One.* If you have this resource, you will want to have it available for the extension activities suggested below.

  Individual and Small Group Study

THE INTRODUCTION

Planning an introduction to guided reading is a complex process. Consider both what a text demands of your readers and what your readers are able to do to process the text efficiently. You need to strike a delicate balance between providing enough support for readers to efficiently process the instructional level text, while also leaving a few opportunities for problem solving.

To begin this study, we recommend watching again the introduction to one of the guided reading lessons you have already viewed.

As you view the introduction to the guided reading lesson:

■ Notice how the teacher in the segment you are viewing strikes the balance between providing support and allowing opportunities for problem solving. Remember to preview the text analyses in Figures 8.2 through 8.9 for the texts used in the guided reading lessons to help you think about the demands of the texts on the readers and how the readers might have been supported.

 Individual Study

1. Select a leveled book for one of your guided reading groups. Using the text analysis form found in PDF Resources and the *Selecting Texts* section of the Guided Reading continuum, analyze the text's characteristics. Which characteristics will be supportive for your readers? Which characteristics will place demands on your readers' processing?

2. Now, turn to the *Selecting Goals* section and select a few of the behaviors and understandings you will want to support your readers in thinking within, beyond, and about the text.

3. Write an introduction to the book you have selected. Remember you will want it to be brief and engaging. Think about the readers you will be working with. Determine the level of support you will want to provide. How will you strike the balance between providing support and allowing for problem solving?

4. Try your book introduction with a group of students.

5. Reflect on what happened:

   ■ How did your introduction support your readers?

   ■ What behaviors and understandings did they demonstrate as readers?

   ■ What do you need to teach them how to do?

 Small Group & Large Group

1. Provide a range of texts leveled from A to L to groups of four to six people. If possible, do not provide the levels on the books. Have the group look at the characteristics of the books and order them from easiest to hardest. Then, reveal the levels and talk about what factors they used in deciding where the texts belonged.

2. Have partners select a book to analyze more deeply using the Text Analysis Form provided under PDF Resources. Using the *Selecting Texts* section of the Guided Reading continuum for the text level of the book they have selected, have them analyze the characteristics of the text. Ask them to talk in partners about the demands of this text on readers.

3. After they have completed the text analysis, have them talk to their partner about the group of readers with whom they plan to use this book. Describe their strengths and areas they are working on as readers. Ask them to talk about which characteristics of the text they have analyzed will be particularly demanding.

4. Have them look in the Guided Reading continuum under *Selecting Goals*. Choose a couple of bullets you think would be appropriate to teach or support during the guided reading lesson.

5. In partners, plan a text introduction using the selected behaviors and understandings as a guide.

6. Ask partners to role-play the introduction in front of their colleagues. Have colleagues think about and discuss the level of support offered in the introduction. What behaviors and understandings were supported or explicitly taught?

READING THE TEXT

Some of your most powerful instruction comes in the brief interactions you have with your students while they are reading the text during a guided reading lesson. It is important to think about the levels of support you provide during this part of the lesson. The Guided Reading continuum can help you hone in on what behaviors and understandings the reader is demonstrating and what behaviors and understandings you may need to teach or support. *Prompting Guide, Part One* provides you with the language you can use to teach, prompt, or reinforce these behaviors. If you have this resource, try the following activity to extend your understanding:

 Individual, Small Group & Large Group

1. Choose one of the guided reading lessons to watch for a second time.

2. After watching the introduction, focus on the part of the lesson in which the children are reading the text.

3. Record the precise language the teacher uses during these interactions to help students problem-solve.

4. After watching the video, think about the levels of support offered by the teacher. Identify the behavior or understanding she was teaching for, prompting for, or reinforcing. Turn to the section of the *Prompting Guide* that corresponds with that behavior and understanding. Talk in your group about the language she used.

- Was she teaching for that behavior and understanding, prompting the students to tap into something they already know how to do, or reinforcing a behavior they noticed?

- What do you think informed her decision to provide the level of support she did?

- How did she translate the bullets from the Guided Reading continuum into language that can be used in instruction?

 Small Group & Large Group

5. If you are working in a group, choose a few bullet points from the Guided Reading continuum and think about how they might sound in instruction. How would it sound if you were teaching for this behavior? How would it sound if you were prompting or reinforcing this behavior?

Give It a Try ▷

Individual Study

1. Choose a group of students who are reading around the same instructional level. Gather their most current reading assessments (running records, Benchmark Assessment, any formal or informal assessments you use to know your readers). Analyze the assessments using the Guided Reading continuum as a tool (see DVD 1: Introduction and Assessment, for more information about how to use the Guided Reading continuum to analyze reading records). Determine what behaviors and understandings your readers understand and areas in which they need growth using the *Selecting Goals* section for the text level that seems instructional for those readers.

2. Select a text for the group that you know will be engaging and instructional for those readers. Briefly review it using the *Selecting Texts* section of the Guided Reading continuum for the appropriate text level, thinking about the text characteristics outlined in this section. Determine the potential supports and demands of this text on your readers.

3. Turn to the *Selecting Goals* section of the Guided Reading continuum. Choose two or three behaviors and understandings you know you will need to support or explicitly teach during your text introduction keeping in mind what you know about the text and the readers. Look over the word work at the bottom of the *Selecting Goals* section to determine what type of word work you might do with the group at the end of the lesson.

4. Plan a text introduction, some possible discussion points for the discussion, and word work for the end of the lesson.

5. Try the lesson with the group.

6. Reflect on what they demonstrated as readers and what you will need to teach them how to do next as readers.

 Small Group & Large Group

1. Follow the steps above.

2. Have teachers share how the Guided Reading continuum helped in their planning and implementation of guided reading in their classrooms.

Translations and Dictations for Student Writing Samples

The dictations below correspond to the writing samples that are available on **DVD 6: Writing: Focus on Writing Workshop,** under PDF Resources. The dictations are available for only the earliest writing as the other samples are legible. The dictations below represent the way the writers read their pieces to their teachers.

Title of Piece	Dictation
PreK: Water Park (Narrative)	"I went to the water park." Words written on piece: Me, San (Sand), wr (water). Tyler explained that the swirled drawing is a water slide.
PreK: Sun and Tree (Functional/Labels)	Labels: sun=sun tree=tree me=me MaCKc=Michael We do not know what *conn* represents on the right hand side of the page.
PreK: Christmas List (Functional/Lists and Procedures)	Elliott's Christmas List PLA DO=Playdough LIT BRIT=Light Bright MR TRK=Monster Truck BAB FR MALLORY=Baby for Mallory DEL SMI=Diesel Semi
Kindergarten: Brady's Birthday (Narrative)	Dictation: It was my birthday and my friends were over. I was turning five.
Kindergarten: *All About Snakes* (Informational/ Literary Nonfiction)	**Dictations** Page 1: The snake shoots poison. Page 2: It is squeezing me. Page 3: It is eating a mouse. Page 4: It went to sleep.
Kindergarten: Things I Like to Do (Functional/ Lists and Procedures)	**Dictations** Page 1: Golf by a waterfall Page 2: Playground Page 3: Corn Maze Page 4: Basketball

DVD at-a-Glance

Titles	Description
INTRODUCTION	
Introduction to the Teaching Library (3:57)	In this segment, the authors explain how the videos relate to *The Continuum of Literacy Learning*. We describe the various instructional contexts presented on the DVDs.
The Design of the Continuum (6:05)	The authors explain why they created *The Continuum of Literacy Learning* and how it can help teachers. They guide you through the text's structure and the organization of the continua.
How to Use the DVD Collection (2:16)	The DVDs may be used by individuals or groups as a tool to plan for and guide teaching. A suggested sequence of study is outlined here and used throughout the User Guide.
ASSESSMENT	
The Values of Assessment (1:53)	The authors explain authentic assessment and its impact on teaching.
Analyzing Individual Reading Behaviors (2:39)	The authors describe the organization of the 12 systems of strategic actions into behaviors for thinking within, beyond, and about the text.
Level C—*Socks* (12:49)	Tarik reads the level C *Benchmark Assessment System* text *Socks*. You can create your own running record of this reading or follow along with a completed record to determine this reader's behaviors.
Level D— *Our Teacher Mr. Brown* (20:43)	Richard reads the level D *Benchmark Assessment System* text *Our Teacher Mr. Brown.* You can create your own running record of this reading or follow along with a completed record to determine this reader's behaviors.
Level J— *Our New Neighbors* (20:37)	Glory reads the level J *Benchmark Assessment System* text *Our New Neighbors*. You can create your own running record of this reading or follow along with a completed record to determine this reader's behaviors.

continues

DVD at-a-Glance, *cont.*

Titles	Description
INTERACTIVE READ-ALOUD AND LITERATURE DISCUSSION	
Introduction (2:14)	The introduction provides an overview of organization of the Interactive Read-Aloud and Literature Discussion continuum and how it can be used to help students talk and think about texts in a variety of ways.
Kindergarten— *Ask Nicely* (10:12)	In this segment, a teacher reads the fiction text *Ask Nicely* to her kindergarten class. The children bring background knowledge to the text, infer characters' feelings, interpret illustrations, and learn new vocabulary, among other things.
Grade 1— *One Tiny Turtle* (19:21)	A class of first graders listens to their teacher read *One Tiny Turtle*, a nonfiction text. They learn about the structure of the text, notice new information, and actively engage in talking and listening.
Grade 1— *My Best Friend* (16:04)	These first graders participate in an interactive read-aloud of the fiction text, *My Best Friend*. The children make predictions, infer the characters' feelings, and make connections to their own lives.
Grade 1— *Chester's Way* (20:11)	The teacher reads the fiction text *Chester's Way* to her first-grade class. They make connections to other texts, make predictions, and compare and contrast characters.
Grade 2— *Grandma's Purple Flowers* (15:03)	Second graders listen to the fiction text *Grandma's Purple Flowers*, talk about the writer's craft, interpret illustrations, and infer characters' feelings.
LITERATURE DISCUSSION	
Grade 1— *Julius, the Baby of the World* (16:37)	A group of first graders discuss the fiction text *Julius, the Baby of the World*. They connect the problems in the story to their own lives and offer evidence to support their thinking about characters' feelings and intentions.
Grade 2— *Roller Coaster* (23:11)	In this segment, a second grade group participates in their first book club. As they discuss the book, *Roller Coaster*, they make personal connections to the topic, describe the plot, and examine the writer's craft and character change.

continues

DVD at-a-Glance, *cont.*

Titles	Description
SHARED AND PERFORMANCE READING	
Introduction (1:47)	The authors describe the characteristics of shared and performance reading and explain how the Continuum can be used to help teachers select texts and goals to support the reading process through this instructional context.
Prekindergarten— *Spots, Feathers, and Curly Tails* (15:05)	A group of prekindergarten students reads the picture book *Spots, Feathers, and Curly Tails.* They search for and use information in the illustrations, learn new vocabulary, and begin to notice visual aspects of print.
Kindergarten— "Here Are My Eyes" (7:38)	Kindergarten students read the poem "Here Are my Eyes." They work on voice-print matching and quickly locating high-frequency words.
Grade 1— *The Enormous Watermelon* (25:05)	First grade students read from the big book *The Enormous Watermelon.* They interpret illustrations, make predictions, look for vowel patterns, and become more efficient word-solvers by breaking down longer words.
WRITING ABOUT READING	
Introduction (3:41)	The authors discuss the value of writing about reading and how a teacher can support students as they compose their responses to texts. They also explain the organization of this continuum in the *Continuum of Literacy Learning.*
Kindergarten— *The Snowy Day* (13:40)	Kindergarten students write about what a character in *The Snowy Day* sees throughout the book. The children notice visual patterns in words and make connections between words.
Kindergarten— *Tops and Bottoms* (20:39)	Kindergarten students think about a story their class read previously during interactive read-aloud and write advice to one of the characters in the book, *Tops and Bottoms.* Students practice the format of a letter and try several word-solving strategies.

continues

DVD at-a-Glance, *cont.*

Titles	Description
Grade 1— *Sheila Rae, the Brave* (14:01)	A first-grade class writes a response to *Sheila Rae, the Brave*. As they write a letter to the main character of the story, they have the opportunity to think about the events of the story and what the character should have done differently.
Grade 1— The Moon (23:41)	First graders in this class write a sentence that explains two things they learned about the moon from their reading. In the segment, they work with words that have two vowels in the middle of them and break down two-syllable words.

WRITING: FOCUS ON INTERACTIVE WRITING

Introduction (4:46)	The authors explain the organization of the Writing continuum, how writers evolve over time, and what teachers can do to help them grow. They define the writing process and the structure of writing workshop.
Prekindergarten Interactive Writing Lesson— Captions for Self-Portraits (16:22)	A group of prekindergarteners work on a simple form of interactive writing—the writing of their names. They are working on connecting beginning sounds to letters.
Kindergarten— Writing About a Brooder (20:58)	These kindergarten students determine and write a sentence about putting chicks in a brooder. They connect new words to known words, learn that two letters can represent one sound, and engage in early reading behaviors.
Kindergarten— Writing a How-To Text (15:44)	The students in this kindergarten class write a how-to text together about making a bird feeder with a bagel. They recall the steps required to make the feeder and work to put the information in a sequence.
Grade 1— Writing About Plants (14:42)	In this segment, the teacher works with a small group of first graders to write about what they have learned about plants. The segment demonstrates how to use the Writing continuum to plan instruction for small groups to teach students about craft, conventions, and the writing process.

continues

DVD at-a-Glance, *cont.*

Titles	Description
WRITING: FOCUS ON WRITING WORKSHOP	
Prekindergarten—Writing Workshop on Bookmaking	
Minilesson (12:09)	A group of four-year-olds learn how to make a book about animals based on a mentor text. The book includes pictures of animals and descriptions of the sounds they make. The students learn about letter-sound relationships.
Conferences (6:46)	In conferences, the students work on sequencing events and recognizing where information is missing.
Grade 1—Writing Workshop on Using Headings	
Minilesson (17:34)	The teacher introduces her first graders to using headings to organize informational writing. She shows them mentor texts and helps them see how headings can guide readers.
Conference with Alison (7:47)	The teacher works with Alison on her informational text about Martin Luther King. They look at a timeline as a tool for finding information, and add headings to the text.
Conference with Sana (6:43)	The teacher works with Sana on how to write headings to organize her writing and then helps her think about how she will revise the piece.
Share (7:21)	The teacher shares several examples from her students' work to reinforce their understanding of the use of headings.
Grade 1—Writing Workshop on Writing How-To Books	
Minilesson (18:52)	This minilesson is about writing "how-to" books— a sequence of directions for how to do something. One boy offers his writing as a model for the class to discuss the process.
Conference with Clementine (7:31)	The teacher works with Clementine on her how-to book about making an egg-carton caterpillar. Clementine revises her piece by adding missing information. The writing piece discussed in this conference is available to print from the DVD under the heading *PDF Resources*.

continues

DVD at-a-Glance, *cont.*

Titles	Description
Conference with Kaya (8:17)	The teacher works with Kaya on revising her how-to book about making a cake. Kaya works on being more specific in her instructions.
Share (9:39)	The student who shared his writing in the minilesson does so again during the share. The class helps him to determine if any information is missing.
Grade 1—Writing Workshop on Adding Important Details	
Minilesson (12:08)	This minilesson for first graders focuses on how to revise writing by adding important details to help readers understand a story. One student's writing serves as a model. Students are then asked to apply the principle to their own writing during writing workshop.
Conference with Isabelle (8:33)	The teacher confers with Isabelle about adding details to her story. Isabelle determines where the information should go in her piece.
Conference with Molly (12:22)	The teacher works with Molly on how to revise her writing to focus on the most important information for her reader.
Conference with Evan (8:19)	The teacher helps Evan think about revising his writing to include more details for his readers.
Share (10:31)	One student shares her writing as the teacher helps her, and the class reflects on the day's minilesson through their feedback.
Grade 1—Writing Workshop on Writing Leads	
Minilesson (7:59)	This minilesson for first graders focuses on how to write a lead for a story. The teacher presents model texts and they discuss why a strong lead is important. Students are asked to read over and revise the leads of their own stories to make sure they engage the reader.
Conference with Nicholas (4:16)	The teacher confers with Nicholas about the lead for a story about his bike. He compares his previous lead with his new one.
Conference with John (8:21)	In this segment, the teacher works with John on a lead for a story about a camping trip.

continues

DVD at-a-Glance, *cont.*

Titles	Description
Conference with Morgan (13:50)	Morgan thinks about what will be most important in her story about Christmas presents. The teacher helps her focus on a small part of her story to help her expand the details.
Share (8:15)	The teacher reiterates the purpose of the lead in a story and has one child read her story to the others. The students' comments help the child to understand what she is communicating in her writing.
Grade 2—Writing Workshop on "Show, Don't Tell"	
Minilesson (10:55)	In this minilesson, the teacher helps her second graders learn that writers show their feelings through descriptions rather than simply telling what they are feeling. The teacher uses her own writing as a model.
Conferences with Anthony, Willy, and Bryn (24:09)	The teacher confers with three students in a row about applying the minilesson principle to their own writing.
Share (17:28)	Bryn shares her story with the class to illustrate the minilesson principle. The students point out the words she used to show her feelings.
PHONICS, SPELLING, AND WORD STUDY	
Introduction (2:42)	The authors explain the organization of the Phonics, Spelling, and Word Study continuum and the nine areas of learning.
Prekindergarten— Name Chart (11:11)	The teacher works with a group of prekindergarten students, helping them notice features of their names. They use the name chart to make connections between the first letters in their names and other words.
Prekindergarten— Name Puzzles (4:06)	In this segment, prekindergarteners learn how to use name puzzles. They put the letters of their names together to form the word and then check it carefully.
Prekindergarten— Magnetic Letters (4:23)	The teacher works with a small group of prekindergarten students to notice the features of letters. They sort magnetic letters into groups—those with circles and those with lines.

continues

DVD at-a-Glance, *cont.*

Titles	Description
Grade 1—Word Parts (14:42)	In this segment students are learning to take words apart using the onset and rime.
Grade 1—Plurals (16:36)	In this segment the teacher gives a phonics/word study minilesson on plurals. The teacher uses simple, known words as examples. Students work with magnetic letters to add an *s* to a word. Then they use the word in a sentence.
Grade 1—Word Endings (10:52)	These first-grade students work on adding *–ed* to words. They work with words they know and learn that the ending has several sounds.
Grade 1—Contractions (20:29)	In this lesson, first-grade students work with examples of *am, is,* and *will* contractions. Then they play the game Concentration, matching contractions with the two words they represent.
Grade 2—Silent Consonants (9:36)	The teacher helps students understand which words have silent consonants. The teacher and the students offer examples of such words in given categories.
Grade 2—Letter-Sound Relationships (7:48)	The teacher helps students notice and use the onset and rime in one-syllable words to help read, write, and spell them.

GUIDED READING

Introduction (5:27)	The authors provide an overview of the structure of a guided reading lesson and explain the organization of the Guided Reading continuum.
Level C—*Clean My Teeth* (15:41)	A kindergarten teacher provides a supportive introduction to this level C text as she points out some of the vocabulary and challenging language structure. Among other things, children learn to use a known word to monitor their reading.
Level F—*Tim's Favorite Toy* (15:23)	A first-grade group reading a level F fiction book discusses the idea of favorite toys. The teacher uses the language of the text in her introduction of the book. After reading the text, they discuss cause and effect.

continues

DVD at-a-Glance, *cont.*

Titles	Description
Level G— *Locked Out* (28:16)	This group of first graders is reading a level G fiction book. They discuss personal experiences and work on fluency.
Level G— *How Animals Move* (24:29)	The teacher helps first graders to notice how the writer has organized the text. After reading, the students discuss some of the new information they encountered. The teacher helps them to realize that they can look at the parts of longer words in order to solve them.
Level K— *Lions and Tigers* (35:53)	This first-grade group reads a level K nonfiction book about lions and tigers, and the teacher introduces them to some of the technical words they will encounter during the reading. They also go over the structure of this informational text, and focus on plurals during word work.
Level K— *Classroom Pets* (36:29)	In this first-grade group, students read a Level K book about pets that are appropriate to have in classrooms. They make predictions about the animals they will encounter in the book and what makes them good classroom pets. The teacher also helps them understand the different meanings of homophones.
Level K— *Emergency Vehicles* (25:49)	This first-grade group reads a level K nonfiction text about different kinds of emergency vehicles. The teacher introduces the different types of emergencies that the book details. They use the introduction of the book to get an overview before reading on their own, and use the table of contents and graphic features to understand the text.
Level K— *Frog and Toad Are Friends* (33:28)	This second-grade group is reading a fiction story with familiar characters. They work on reading with expression and making sure their reading makes sense. After reading, they discuss the turning point in the story.

References

Pinnell, G.S., and I.C. Fountas. 2011, 2008. *The Continuum of Literacy Learning, Grades PreK–8: A Guide to Teaching*. Portsmouth, NH: Heinemann.

Fountas, I.C., and G.S. Pinnell. 2010. *Fountas and Pinnell Benchmark Assessment System 1: Grades K–2, Levels A–N*. Portsmouth, NH: Heinemann.

Pinnell, G.S. and Fountas, I.C. 2009. *When Readers Struggle: Teaching that Works.* Portsmouth, NH: Heinemann.

Fountas, I.C., and G.S. Pinnell. 2008. *The Fountas and Pinnell Prompting Guide, Part 1: A Tool for Literacy Teachers*. Portsmouth, NH: Heinemann.

Fountas, I.C., and G.S. Pinnell. 2006. *Teaching for Comprehending and Fluency: Thinking, Talking, and Writing about Reading, K–8*. Portsmouth, NH: Heinemann.

Pinnell, G.S. and Fountas, I.C. 2002. *Phonics Lessons: Letters, Words, and How They Work, Grades K–2*. Portsmouth, NH: Heinemann.

Fountas, I.C., and G.S. Pinnell. 2001. *Guiding Readers and Writers: Teaching Comprehension, Genre, and Content Literacy*. Portsmouth, NH: Heinemann.

McCarrier, A., Pinnell, G.S., and Fountas, I.C. 1999. *Interactive Writing: How Language and Literacy Come Together, K–2*. Portsmouth, NH: Heinemann.

Pinnell, G.S. and Fountas, I.C. 1998. *Word Matters: Teaching Phonics and Spelling in the Reading/Writing Classroom.* Portsmouth, NH: Heinemann.

Fountas, I.C., and G.S. Pinnell. 1996. *Guided Reading: Good First Teaching for All Children*. Portsmouth, NH: Heinemann.

Video Credits

The following texts were used in the video segments with permission from the publishers:

Spots, Feathers and Curly Tails by Nancy Tafuri. Used by permission of HarperCollins Publishers.

Grandma's Purple Flowers © 2000 by Adjoa J. Burrowes. Permission arranged with Lee & Low Books, Inc. New York, NY 10016.

Chester's Way by Kevin Henkes. Copyright © 1988 by Kevin Henkes. Used by permission of HarperCollins Publishers.

The Snowy Day by Ezra Jack Keats. Copyright © 1962 by Ezra Jack Keats, renewed © 1990 by Martin Pope, Executor. Presented by special permission from the Ezra Jack Keats Foundation.

My Best Friend by Mary Ann Rodman, illustrated by E.B. Lewis. Text copyright © Mary Ann Rodman, 2005. Illustrations copyright © E.B. Lewis, 2005. Text used by permission of Puffin Books, an imprint of Penguin Young Readers Group, a division of Penguin Group (USA) Inc. Illustrations used by permission of Dwyer & O'Grady Inc.

The Enormous Watermelon retold by Brenda Parkes and Judith Smith, illustrated by Mary Davy. Copyright © 1997 Mimosa Publications. Used by permission of McGraw-Hill International.

One Tiny Turtle. Text copyright © 2001 by Nicola Davies. Illustrations copyright © 2001 by Jane Chapman. Reproduced by permission of the publisher, Candlewick Press, Somerville, MA, on behalf of Walker Books, London.

Ask Nicely! By Pauline Cartwright; illustrated by Martin Bailey. Used by permission of Pearson Australia.

Lions and Tigers (New PM Story Books), by Beverly Randell. Melbourne: © 1998. Cengage Learning Australia, a part of Cengage Learning, Inc. Used with permission.

Coding and Scoring Errors at-a-Glance

Behavior	What the Reader Does	How to Code	Example	How to Score	
Accurate Reading	Reads words correctly	Do not mark or place check (✓) above word.	no mark or $\dfrac{✓}{\text{Kate}}$		No error
Substitution	Gives an incorrect response.	Write the substituted word above the word.	$\dfrac{\text{her}}{\text{Kate's}}$	Substitution, not corrected	1 error
				Substitution, selfcorrected (SC)	No error; 1 SC
Multiple Substitutions	Makes several attempts at a word	Write each of the substitutions in sequence above the word.	$\dfrac{\text{little\|some\|him}}{\text{his}}$	Multiple substitutions, not corrected	1 error for each incorrect word in text
			$\dfrac{\text{touch\|teeth\|SC}}{\text{tooth}}$	Multiple substitutions, self-corrected (SC)	No error; 1 SC
			$\dfrac{\text{to\|touch\|teeth}}{\text{tooth}}$	Multiple misreadings of the same word not corrected	1 error for each incorrect word in text
			$\dfrac{\text{Kathy\|Kelly}}{\text{Kate}}$	Multiple misreadings of names and proper nouns	1 error first time missed; no errors after that
			$\dfrac{\text{It's}}{\text{It is}}$ $\dfrac{\text{Do not}}{\text{Don't}}$	Misreading contractions (reads contraction as two words or two words as contraction)	1 error each time
Self-correction	Corrects a previous error	Write the error over the word, followed by SC.	$\dfrac{\text{\|teeth\|SC}}{\text{tooth}}$		No error; 1 SC
Insertion	Adds a word that is not in the text	Write in the inserted word using a carat (^).	loose ⌃		1 error per word inserted
Omission	Gives no response to a word	Place a dash (–) above the word.	$\dfrac{\text{—}}{\text{Very}}$	Skipping a word	1 error per word
				Skipping a line	1 error per word
Repetition	Reads the same word again	Write R above the word.	R		No error

Coding and Scoring Errors at-a-Glance, *cont.*

Behavior	What the Reader Does	How to Code	Example	How to Score	
Repeated Repetitions	Reads the same word more than once	Write R above the word for the first repetition and then write a number for the additional repetitions.	R₂ R₃		No error
Rereading	Returns to the beginning of sentence or phrase to read again	Write R with an arrow back to the place where rereading began.	R		No error
	Rereads and selfcorrects	Write R with an arrow back to the place where rereading began and SC at point of self-correction	R tooth to come|SC tooth to fall		No error; 1 SC
Appeal	Verbally asks for help	Write A above the word.	$\frac{A}{Very}$	Follow up with "You try it."	No error
"You Try It"	The child appeals, the teacher responds with "You try it."	Write Y after the word.	$\frac{A}{very}$ | Y	You try it" followed by correct word	No error
				"You try it" followed by omission, incorrect word, or Told	1 error
Told	Child doesn't attempt word even after "You try it."	Write T after the word or the Y.	$\frac{A}{very}$|Y|T $\frac{A}{very}$|T		1 error
Spelling Aloud	The child spells the word by saying the names of letters.	Write the letters in all capital letters.	$\frac{B\text{-}U\text{-}T}{But}$	Spelling followed by correct word	No error
				Spelling followed by incorrect word	1 error
Sounding Out	The child makes the sounds associated with the letters in the word.	Write the letters in lowercase with hyphens between them.	$\frac{n\text{-}o\text{-}t}{not}$ $\frac{l\text{-}o\text{-}s}{loose}$ | lose $\frac{f\text{-}}{come}$ | SC	"Sounding out" followed by correct word	No error; no SC
				"Sounding out" followed by incorrect word	1 error
				Sounding the first letter incorrectly and then saying the word correctly	No error; 1 SC

Analysis of

_____ Level _____)

Text Factor	Analysis
Genre	
Text Structure	
Content	
Themes and Ideas	
Language and	
Literary Features	
Sentence Complexity	
Vocabulary	
Words	
Illustrations	
Book and Print Features	

When introducing this text in guided reading, keep this in mind:

Analyzing Reading Behaviors
Using the Guided Reading Continuum

Student Name	Behaviors and Understandings the Student Demonstrates	Behaviors and Understandings to Teach and Support

Observing Writing About Reading

Behaviors and Understandings to Notice, Teach, and Support

Understandings About the Genre or Form	Understandings About Phonics, Spelling, and Word Study	Evidence of Behaviors and Understandings	Behaviors and Understandings the Teacher is Supporting

Analyzing Writing About Reading

Title of Writing Piece	Genre and Form	Behaviors and Understandings Evidenced in the Writing (From the Writing About Reading Continuum)	Next Steps

Using the Continuum to Assess Student Writing

Genre	Craft	Conventions	Writing Process
Behaviors and Understandings the Student Demonstrates			
Evidence of Behaviors and Understandings			
Next Steps			

Guide for Observing and Noting Reading Behaviors	C P N	Notes
1. Early Reading Behaviors *Does the reader:* • Move left to right across a line of print? • Return to the left for a new line? • Match voice to print while reading a line or more of print? • Recognize a few easy high-frequency words?		
2. Searching for and Using Information **Meaning** *Does the reader:* • Make meaningful attempts at unknown words? • Use the meaning of the story or text to predict unknown words? • Reread to gather more information to solve a word? • Reread and use the meaning of the sentence? • Reread to search for more details—information, characters, plot? • Reread to gather information to clarify confusions? • Use headings and titles to think about the meaning of a section of text? • Use information in the pictures to help in understanding a text? • Use knowledge of the genre (and its characteristics) to help in understanding a text? • Use knowledge of the genre (and its characteristics) to help in finding information? • Use readers' tools to help in finding information (glossary, index)? **Structure** *Does the reader:* • Use knowledge of oral language to solve unknown words? • Reread to see if a word "sounds right" in a sentence? • Reread to correct using language structure? **Visual Information** *Does the reader:* • Use the visual information to solve words? • Use the sound of the first letter(s) to attempt or solve a word? • Use some, most, or all of the visual information to solve words? • Use sound analysis to solve a word? • Make attempts that are visually similar? • Use knowledge of a high-frequency word to problem solve? • Search for more visual information within a word to solve it? • Use analogy to solve unknown words?		

Guide for Observing and Noting Reading Behaviors, *cont.*	C P N	Notes
Visual Information, *cont.* *Does the reader:* • Use syllables to solve words? • Use prefixes and suffixes to take apart and recognize words? • Use inflectional endings to problem solve words? • Recognize words quickly and easily? • Reread and use the sound of the first letter to solve a word? • Problem solve unknown words quickly and efficiently? • Work actively to solve words? • Use multiple sources of information together in attempts at words? • Use all sources of information flexibly to solve words? • Use all sources of information in an orchestrated way?		
3. Solving Words *Does the reader:* • Recognize a core of high-frequency words quickly? • Recognize words quickly and easily? • Use a variety of flexible ways to take words apart? • Use the meaning of the sentences to solve words? • Use the structure of the sentence to solve words? • Use some of the visual information to solve words? • Use known word parts to solve words? • Use sound analysis (sounding out)? • Use analogy to solve words? • Make attempts that are visually similar? • Use the sound of the first letter to solve words? • Work actively to solve words? • Use known words or parts to solve unknown words? • Use syllables to problem solve? • Use prefixes and suffixes to take words apart? • Use inflectional endings to take words apart? • Use sentence context to derive the meaning of words? • Use base words and root words to derive the meaning of words? • Make connections among words to understand their meaning?		
4. Self-Monitoring *Does the reader:* • Hesitate at an unknown word? • Stop at an unknown word? • Stop at an unknown word and appeal for help? • Stop after an error?		

Guide for Observing and Noting Reading Behaviors, *cont.*	C P N	Notes
4. Self-Monitoring, cont. *Does the reader:* • Notice mismatches? • Notice when an attempt does not look right? • Notice when an attempt does not sound right? • Notice when an attempt does not make sense? • Reread to confirm reading? • Use knowledge of some high-frequency words to check on reading? • Check one source of information with another? • Check an attempt that makes sense with language? • Check an attempt that makes sense with the letters (visual information)? • Use language structure to check on reading? • Request help after making several attempts?		
5. Self-Correcting *Does the reader:* • Reread and try again until accurate? • Stop after an error and make another attempt? • Stop after an error and make multiple attempts until accurate? • Reread to self-correct? • Work actively to solve mismatches? • Self-correct errors?		
6. Maintaining Fluency *Does the reader:* • Read without pointing? • Read word groups (phrases)? • Put words together? • Read smoothly? • Read the punctuation? • Make the voice go down at periods? • Make the voice go up at question marks? • Pause briefly at commas, dashes, and hyphens? • Read dialogue with intonation or expression? • Stress the appropriate words to convey accurate meaning? • Read at a good rate—not too fast and not too slow?		
7. Other Behaviors		